מסורה

ArtScroll Youth Series®

The Story of
The Chofetz Chaim

The Story of

by
Rabbi Nosson Scherman
and
Rabbi Eliezer Gevirtz

illustrated by
Yosef Dershowitz
Designed by
Sheah Brander

The
Chofetz Chaim

Published by

Mesorah Publications, ltd

in conjunction with
Torah Umesorah
National Society for Hebrew Day Schools

FIRST EDITION
First Impression ... July, 1983

Published and Distributed by
MESORAH PUBLICATIONS, Ltd.
1969 Coney Island Avenue
Brooklyn, New York 11223

Also available to schools and students through
TORAH UMESORAH PUBLICATIONS
160 Broadway
New York, N.Y. 10038

Distributed in Israel by
MESORAH MAFITZIM / J. GROSSMAN
Rechov Bayit Vegan 90/5
Jerusalem, Israel

Distributed in Europe by
J. LEHMANN HEBREW BOOKSELLERS
20 Cambridge Terrace
Gateshead, Tyne and Wear
England NE8 1RP

Published in conjunction with
TORAH UMESORAH / National Society for Hebrew Day Schools
160 Broadway, New York, N.Y. 10038

Typography by CompuScribe at ArtScroll Studios, Ltd.
1969 Coney Island Avenue / Brooklyn, N.Y. 11223 / (212) 339-1700

Printed in U.S.A. by
EDISON LITHOGRAPHING AND PRINTING CORP.

◆§ Preface

בס"ד

Few people's names in recent times are uttered with as much awe and admiration as that of the legendary *Chofetz Chaim,* Rabbi Yisroel Meir HaKohain Kagan זצ"ל. The mere mention of his name evokes feelings of *kedushah* and a desire to strive for sanctity and greater heights in Torah and *yiras shamayim.*

If the above holds true with a mere mention of the name, how much more can be realized by reading an entire book that details episodes in the life of this great *tzaddik* and sage, from his early childhood to his passing.

It is for this purpose that the Torah Umesorah Publications Department together with Mesorah Publications undertook the publication of *The Story of the Chofetz Chaim.*

It is our hope and prayer that as adults and children read about the *Chofetz Chaim's* life; its events will become inscribed in their *neshamos* and will stay with them for the rest of their lives, instilling in them the ambition to go from strength to strength — to grow spiritually and physically during *their* lifetimes, just as the *Chofetz Chaim* did during *his* lifetime.

We are indebted to the authors, Rabbi Nosson Scherman and Rabbi Eliezer Gevirtz, who diligently gave of their time and talents to cull through the source material available on the life of the *Chofetz Chaim,* and produce a book that is suitable for readers of all ages.

The entire staff of Mesorah Publications, and Yosef Dershowitz who illustrated the book, are to be commended for producing another product לְשֵׁם וּלְתִפְאֶרֶת.

We wish to express words of gratitude to our dear friend, David M. Singer, Chairman of Torah Umesorah's Executive Committee, for his encouragement and support for the publication of this work.

Reb Dovid, an exemplary *askan* for Torah, personifies in word and deed the teachings of the *Chofetz Chaim.* His character, sincerity, and *emunas chachamim* serve as a model for all of us to emulate.

In merit of his indefatiguable work for הַחֲזָקַת הַתּוֹרָה may he and his wife be granted continued *nachas* from their children, and the blessing of בָּרוּךְ אֲשֶׁר יָקִים אֶת דִּבְרֵי הַתּוֹרָה הַזֹּאת.

It is our fervent hope that the *zechus* of the *Chofetz Chaim,* who's fiftieth *yahrzeit* we commemorate this year, will stand by us during these difficult *galus* times, and that in the merit of bringing our people closer to the ways of our Torah, we be privileged to greet מָשִׁיחַ צִדְקֵנוּ בִּמְהֵרָה בְיָמֵינוּ.

Rabbi Yaakov Fruchter
Director, Torah Umesorah Publications

Sivan 5743

⪧ Author's Acknowledgements

The legacy of the *Chofetz Chaim* consists of not only his writings and teachings, but also his personal example. His uncompromising honesty and obvious concern for the welfare of others set a standard all of us must strive to reach. My thanks go to many people whose own teachings and personal examples have greatly aided me in my work on this book and throughout my life.

Rabbi Yaakov Fruchter, director of Torah Umesorah Publications, has long helped to make suitable Torah-based literature available for today's Jewish youth. His efforts in this and other projects has been crucial in bringing them to fruition.

The leadership provided by the revered *rabbonim* of *Khal Adas Yeshurun* of Washington Heights, N.Y. — Rav Dr. Joseph Breuer, זצ"ל, and Rav Shimon Schwab שליט"א (who was himself inspired by the *Chofetz Chaim)* — has transmitted the Torah traditions championed by the *Chofetz Chaim* to a new American generation. That generation, including myself, owes them an everlasting debt.

I would also like to express my gratitude to the following *rabbonim,* (listed alphabetically): Rabbis Jacob Breuer, Sheldon Chwat, Shlomoh Danziger, Yonah Fuld, Shimon Herskovits, Eliyohu Krieger, and Menachem Weldler. May their students and colleagues continue to be inspired by their dedication to the Torah ideals they convey so effectively.

My parents, Mr. and Mrs. Sidney Gevirtz; grandparents, Rev. and Mrs. Gershon Gevirtz and Mr. and Mrs. Max Freymark; and aunt and uncle, Mr. and Mrs. Charles Rocoff, have been guiding lights in my life, and their support over the years is deeply appreciated.

Finally, I pay tribute to my students at Yeshiva Rabbi Samson Raphael Hirsch and S.A.R. Academy, and to my nephews and niece, Ely, Dovid, and Aviva Greenberg. May they be inspired by the example of the *Chofetz Chaim* to turn an often corrupt and unfeeling world into a place fit for the arrival of the Mashiach.

Eliezer Gevirtz
Sivan 5743

Historical Note
    Radin (spelled Radun in Polish) is a small village in the region of Grodno, located near the meeting point of the borders of Byelorussia, Lithuania and Poland. Today Radin is a part of Byelorussia, but it was originally a Polish royal estate. In custom and lifestyle the Jews of the region followed the traditions of Lithuanian Jewry.

◄§ Table of Contents

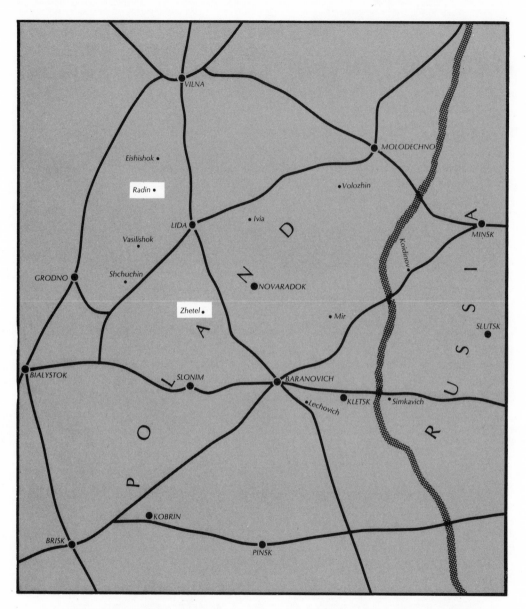

VILNA-MINSK-BRISK AREA IN THE ERA BETWEEN
WORLD WAR I AND WORLD WAR II

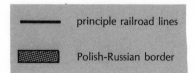

principle railroad lines

Polish-Russian border

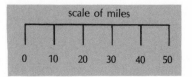

scale of miles

0   10   20   30   40   50

CHAPTER ONE
Are You a Kohain?

A young visitor walked up the narrow street in the small Polish town of Radin. It wasn't much of a town. It wasn't mentioned in any Social Studies textbook; why should it be? There were thousands of unimportant little towns and villages just like it all over Poland. For Jews, however, there was something very, very special about Radin. True, it had a great and famous *yeshivah,* but other cities had great *yeshivos* too. What Radin had was a very great man, a sage and *tzaddik* (righteous man), who was loved and respected by Jews everywhere, and it was him whom the young visitor came to see.

The sage's name was Rabbi Yisroel Meir Hakohain Kagan and he was very, very old — well past ninety. He was quite weak, as you would expect at his age, but his eyes were still young and his mind was as brilliant and alert as it was seventy years earlier. It was then that people had first begun to realize that little Radin had a citizen who would become one of the most famous, important, and beloved Jews on earth.

The visitor that day was a *yeshivah* student from Germany who felt that his Torah education could not be considered complete unless he made a trip to Radin to see — and, if he were fortunate, to speak to — the elderly sage and *tzaddik.*

Reb Yisroel Meir always had people calling on him, to visit, to discuss Torah law, or to ask for advice. He loved people and enjoyed talking to them. It was a strange thing — not only was his wisdom relied upon by the greatest Torah leaders of the age, who seldom made important decisions without consulting him, but even the simple, unlearned working people and tradesmen of Radin loved to visit him and didn't feel uncomfortable in his company.

Most people who didn't know him guessed that he must be a quiet person who spoke very little. That was because his first famous *sefer* (book) was about the laws prohibiting gossip and other kinds of evil speech. In fact, Reb Yisroel Meir was known as the *Chofetz Chaim* all over the world because that was the name of that famous first *sefer*. "A man who is so careful about forbidden speech must do very little talking," thought most people. They were wrong. He did lots of talking, and all honest, sincere people loved talking to him. In fact those who knew him always said that the *Chofetz Chaim* was the best proof of how entertaining and interesting a person could be without ever making other people suffer through mean, nasty or "funny" stories or remarks about them.

As the young German *yeshivah* student made his way down the narrow winding street of Radin that was built to accommodate traffic no heavier than horse-drawn wagons, he wondered what the *Chofetz Chaim* would say to him. After all, the sage was very old and his health wasn't good any more. He might be annoyed at the idea that a stranger was coming to bother him at a stage in life when he had little strength to spare for unimportant intrusions.

There was the house. It was just as the young man had imagined it. Very plain and poor looking. The *Chofetz Chaim* could have lived in a mansion if he had wanted to. If people were told that the beloved sage needed a more comfortable and convenient place to live in his old age, Radin would have been flooded with enough money to build a palace fit for a king. But the *Chofetz Chaim* didn't need a mansion. He didn't even accept a salary from his *yeshivah* even though he started it in his own home and, together with his family, was responsible for training and caring for hundreds of students. The only money he ever accepted was money that he earned through the sales of the many *sefarim* (books) that he had written or, in his younger years, income from the store that his wife operated with a little help from him.

In front of the modest house was a wooden bench. The visitor smiled when he saw it. He remembered a famous picture of the *Chofetz Chaim* sitting on that bench surrounded by members of his family and neighbors. Inside this house would be another few benches like that one and a plain wooden table. The *Chofetz Chaim* didn't believe in beautiful and expensive furniture. Why buy furniture when the money could be put to better use helping Torah scholars, feeding poor people in Poland, Russia or Palestine (as Israel was called in those days), or giving loans to people in temporary financial need? Now, of course, there would be a comfortable easy chair because the *Chofetz Chaim*, in his nineties, could no longer sit on a hard, wooden bench, but that was all.

The student recalled hearing of a wealthy traveler who had come to Radin to visit the famous sage. The well-dressed, free-spending man stepped down from his luxurious coach and entered the home of Radin's most famous citizen. When he saw his humble surrounding, he was astonished! Where was the elegant dining room set? The plush sofa and comfortable chairs? The guest asked, "Rabbi, where is your furniture?"

The sage smiled and asked in return, "Where is yours?"

The wealthy guest was surprised. "I don't understand the question, Rabbi. My furniture is in my home. I am only traveling through Radin!"

"I am also only traveling through. The true home of a Jew is in the World to Come. We travel through this world 'on business' to learn Torah and do the *mitzvos* (good deeds) that will purchase us a good share in the next world. I have no need for furniture here — it would only take away money and energy from more important things."

The German *yeshivah* student entered the home and there before him was the angelic man he had heard so much about and had come so far to see. The *Chofetz Chaim* sat wrapped in his *tallis,* and was wearing *tefillin.* He was studying Torah even though he was one of the greatest Torah scholars of the century. Like all truly great men he knew that the Torah is like an ocean, and that no matter how much someone may know, there is always more to learn, more than he can imagine. He looked up and warmly greeted the young guest.

After asking the young man's name, birthplace, and *yeshivah,* the *Chofetz Chaim* asked, "Are you a *Kohain* (descendant of the priestly family of Aharon [Aaron], brother of Moshe [Moses])?"

"No."

"Why aren't you a *Kohain?*"

"Because my father isn't a *Kohain,*" the young man answered, surprised by the question and thinking that it must be some sort of joke.

"Why isn't your father a *Kohain?*"

"Because my grandfather isn't a *Kohain!*"

"Why isn't your grandfather a *Kohain?*"

The young man didn't answer. He didn't know what to say to questions such as these. They made no sense to him, but could so great a man ask questions that were meaningless? Could it be, he thought, that in the *Chofetz Chaim's* advanced old age, his mind was no longer clear?

The *Chofetz Chaim* noticed his visitor's discomfort. He smiled and explained why he was asking such strange questions. "I am a *Kohain,*" he said, "because my father and his father going all the way back to Aharon were *Kohanim.* Do you know why Aharon and his children became *Kohanim?* Because when Moshe came down from his first forty days on Mount Sinai and found the Jews dancing around the Golden Calf, he called out, 'Whoever is completely loyal to *Hashem,* let him come to me.' Moshe wanted people who were ready to give up everything they had for the sake of *Hashem.* The tribe of Levi stepped forward. The greatest of the *Leviyim* was Aharon; that is why *Hashem* appointed Levi His chosen tribe and Aharon's family His chosen *Kohanim.*

"From that incident over thirty-two centuries ago we learn that when people are courageous and do something out of the ordinary to serve *Hashem,* he rewards them richly. I am a *Kohain* because of something my ancestor Aharon did. Never forget, my son, that *Hashem* remembers and rewards good deeds. Be ambitious to serve *Hashem* and to help Jews — and centuries from now, your deeds will still be rewarded."

The young man looked at the *tzaddik* with new love and respect. Yes, his wisdom and hospitality were just as people said. And his greatness was not only because of something Aharon had done. The *Chofetz Chaim* had accomplished so much in his long, busy life that it would take many, many centuries for him to be repaid. Surely the world was a different and better place because he had lived on it. And that is a statement that could not be made about many people.

CHAPTER TWO
Growing Up Under His Mother's Care

Zhetel, a small town about thirty miles from Vilna, the Lithuanian capital, was the birthplace of little Yisroel Meir Kagan. His father, Rabbi Aryeh Zev, was a quiet, learned, G-d-fearing man who already had children by an earlier marriage. His first wife was still a very young women when she died, and the children were babies. Reb Aryeh Zev married Dobrusha, the younger sister of his first wife. She was only fourteen years old when they were married — early marriages were very common then — but even as a young girl she was unusually mature. Five years later, her first child, Yisroel Meir, was born. She and Reb Aryeh Zev had two other children later on, but both died as infants.

It is hard for us to imagine the poverty of most Eastern European Jews in those days. Most families ate meat only on *Shabbos,* they couldn't afford it any other time; and quite a few families could manage a real meat meal only on a *Yom Tov.* When we hear the word *Kiddush,* we think of a shiny silver cup filled with wine, but in those days many people had to make *Kiddush* on hard black bread because they couldn't afford wine or even white flour for *challah.* It wasn't unusual for children and their parents to go to bed hungry because a hard-working father came home with too little money to buy anything for supper.

The Kagans, too, lived a hard life. Reb Aryeh Zev couldn't make a living in Zhetel. He supported his family by living in "far-off" Vilna — thirty miles was a big distance in the days before cars, trains, and buses. He taught Torah subjects to children of the wealthy Jewish families of Vilna. When his lessons were over he would spend the rest of the day studying Torah in one of Vilna's many study halls. For many centuries, Vilna had been a famous Torah center — it was often called "the Jerusalem of Lithuania" — and the private tutor from little Zhetel was respected as a distinguished scholar. He saved up his earnings from tutoring and turned them over to Dobrusha when he went home to spend some time with his family, but that was seldom more than twice a year, for *Pesach* and *Succos.*

So the responsibility for raising Yisroel Meir fell to Dobrusha — and she was equal to the task. She was an unusual *tzaddekes* (righteous woman). She spent much of her time praying and studying. But, more important for the education of her children, she was as careful as a human being could possibly be to avoid *lashon hara* (evil speech) and idle gossip. So she stayed away from places where people just sit and talk. She used to say, "Loneliness protects the soul's holiness."

She was Yisroel Meir's first *"rebbe,"* and in her old age when the *Chofetz Chaim* was famous as a great *tzaddik* and sage, Dobrusha would proudly tell her friends that it was she who taught him to read. In later years, after Reb Aryeh Zev died and Dobrusha taught reading to her little daughter by a second marriage, she used to tell her sometimes-reluctant student, "If I was a good enough teacher for Yisroel Meir, then I'm certainly a good enough teacher for you."

Even in his later years, when he was known throughout the world, Yisroel Meir never forgot the debt he owed his mother. When he was well past eighty, one of his nephews found Dobrusha's *Tehillim* (Book of Psalms) and, the next time he came to visit the *Chofetz Chaim,* brought him the *Tehillim.*

The old sage's fingers trembled and tears rolled down his cheeks as he lovingly took his late mother's *Tehillim* in his hands. "How can you know how many tears Mother shed over this *Tehillim.* Every morning she would pray that her little boy should grow up to be a G-d-fearing and learned Jew ..."

And he kissed the *Tehillim* and wept.

As soon as Yisroel Meir was old enough, Dobrusha sent him to the little *cheder* (yeshivah for young children) in Zhetel to begin studying *Chumash.* He was a brilliant child and a serious one, too. Not only was he brighter than anyone else, he also tried harder than anyone else. But it was in other ways that he showed himself destined for future greatness.

In the market place of Zhetel there was a poor widow who supported herself by selling apples. One day, when Yisroel Meir was still a pre-school child, he and his friends were roaming around the little town, running and playing. The apple-seller's basket fell over and her apples went rolling in all directions down the street. The boys saw it happen and they scampered after the apples, grabbing them and running away while the poor apple lady screamed after them to stop, but to no avail. Yisroel Meir, too, helped himself to a few apples and ran away as fast as his little legs would carry him. A year or two later he was a *cheder* student and his *rebbe* was teaching the class about the sin of stealing — לֹא תִגְנֹב, "You shall not steal," the Torah says. Yisroel Meir froze in his seat and thought back to what he had done just a few years ago in the Zhetel market place. He had stolen!

As soon as the class was over, Yisroel Meir ran home and asked his mother for a kopeck (a small coin) to buy apples. Dobrusha was a little surprised — Yisroel Meir seldom if ever asked for treats, since he knew there was no money to spare at home — but she gave it to him. He went to the market place and found the apple lady whom he had wronged. He asked for a kopeck's worth of apples. She took the money and handed him a few apples. Yisroel Meir quickly threw the apples back into her basket and ran away before the astonished woman even had a chance to ask him what happened.

That was one side of Yisroel Meir's character. He was, from his earliest youth, always careful to deal honestly and fairly with people. As he grew up and became a businessman, author, publisher, salesman, rabbi, *rosh yeshivah* (seminary dean) and just plain member of the Jewish people, he never forgot that the Torah commands every Jew not to steal and not to desire someone else's property. The tales about his honesty and absolute refusal to profit unfairly at someone else's expense are many and, for most ordinary people, unbelievable.

There were other sides to his character, too. He felt responsible to help others whenever he could. And if he could do it without being known to them, then so much the better. This, too, was a habit he developed in childhood.

There was a water-carrier in Zhetel. In those days before indoor plumbing and running water, one of a family's most important and most bothersome tasks was going to the town well, drawing water, and carrying the heavy buckets back home. Even when waste is kept to an absolute minimum, cooking and washing demand lots of water and, at sixty-two and a half pounds per cubic foot, the job of bringing it is not easy. So it is not surprising that a man who couldn't afford to buy a store, be a merchant, or operate a horse-and-wagon could earn a poor living by delivering water for a few kopecks per bucket. In Zhetel as elsewhere, all he needed was a strong back and two buckets that hung from a rounded stick slung across his shoulders as he grunted and struggled under his burden of a hundred pounds or so, back and forth all day long from pump to home and back again for the next delivery. Weary and exhausted after a long day's work, he would leave his bucket and yoke outside the door of his tiny house overnight.

One day at *cheder,* Yisroel Meir heard his schoolmates

laughing in delight at a "funny trick." In the middle of the frigid Lithuanian winter, several of them filled up the water-carrier's buckets with water. When he woke up in the morning he found his buckets filled with ice! The poor man would have to chop away the ice and not only lose precious time from work, but take the risk of breaking a precious bucket without which his family would go hungry that day. Yisroel Meir was shocked not only at the deed itself, but at his friends' enjoyment of the plight of their victim.

The next morning at *cheder* there was a different topic of conversation. The boys had filled the pails again and, in the morning, they had gathered some distance from the water-carrier's house to watch the fun, but, to their amazement and disappointment, the water-carrier went out his door, put the yoke over his shoulders and went to the well to begin his day's work. No ice! What had happened? The same thing went on for the rest of the winter. No ice. No fun!

What happened was that little Yisroel Meir, without a word to anyone, slipped out of his home after Dobrusha and the older children were asleep and emptied the buckets before the water had time to freeze. No one knew about the solution to "The Mystery of the Empty Buckets" for many, many years. When he was an adult, the *Chofetz Chaim* revealed this secret of his boyhood. By that time, no one was surprised to hear that Reb Yisroel Meir of Radin, world famous sage and *tzaddik,* was not too busy and selfish a child to help a poor, simple water-carrier.

The growing-up years in Zhetel couldn't last. It was too small a town to support a *yeshivah* of the high caliber needed by a genius like Yisroel Meir. His *Gemara* (Talmud) *rebbe,* Reb Moshe Aharon, was a good friend of Yisroel Meir's father, Reb Aryeh Zev, and he kept a close watch over his star student while the boy's father was away in Vilna for months at a time. When the father came home, Reb Moshe Aharon gave him glowing reports on Yisroel Meir's progress in Torah and the observance of *mitzvos,* and urged Reb Aryeh Zev to take the boy along with him to Vilna. There he would be able to enter a *yeshivah* where he would be surrounded by many brilliant students. There he would develop into an outstanding young *talmid chacham* (Torah scholar) thanks to the advantages in Vilna that little Zhetel could never offer.

Reb Aryeh Zev agreed and Yisroel Meir's early boyhood ended. He was only nine years old when his father took him to Vilna.

CHAPTER THREE
Vilna — and Alone

Reb Aryeh Zev and his son, Yisroel Meir, arrived in Vilna in 5607 (1847). The father, proud of his son, took him to one of the famous rabbis of the city to be tested in his knowledge of the Talmud. The rabbi was pleased with the youngster and gave him some advice that Yisroel Meir often repeated in later years:

"You are a fine boy. Don't lose your good name."

The advice was simple enough; every child hears things like that dozens of times during his youth. The *Chofetz Chaim* was unique in that he always saw the wisdom of seemingly simple sayings — and he remembered them, unlike others who retain advice only for as long as it takes to get in one ear and out the other.

Surprisingly, a brilliant young *yeshivah* student in Vilna, the Torah capital of Europe, could very easily lose his good name. The *Maskilim* (so-called "enlightened Jews") were hard at work luring religious Jews, especially promising students, away from Torah study and observance. Young Yisroel Meir became a favorite target of the *Maskilim* not only because of his Talmudic brilliance, but because he was a mathematical genius. Word of the Zheteler *ilui* (genius from Zhetel) spread throughout the city and people often came to visit the study hall where he learned Torah while his father was occupied with his private lessons. The scholars of Vilna came to engage the brilliant youngster in Talmudic discussions while the *Maskilim* came to test his mathematical ability and to convince him to join them. So intense did the pressure from the *Maskilim* become, that Yisroel Meir, at the age of eleven, actually left Vilna and stayed in a nearby town for a while to escape them! Reb Aryeh Zev kept a close watch over his son during the time they were together in Vilna and his vigilance was rewarded as the youngster developed into the city's finest student.

The "big city" children were probably amused at first by the little boy from the little town, to whom Vilna was new and strange. His clothes certainly showed the poverty of his upbringing and it didn't help when he was placed in a study group with older boys. Yisroel Meir had inherited his father's love of learning and his mother's refusal to gossip about people; it didn't take long, therefore, for the other boys to learn that the newcomer was no ordinary child. They began telling their parents about the young genius from Zhetel and, before long, Yisroel Meir Kagan was talked about all over town.

One of those who heard about him was Reb Yisroel Gordon, one of Vilna's wealthiest Orthodox Jews. Reb Yisroel was himself a Torah scholar of note and he was head of a family that had been famous for centuries. His son, Mordechai, was a friend of Yisroel Meir. When Mr. Gordon heard about the boy, he saw an opportunity to kill two birds with one stone. He wanted a good friend, study companion, and "brother" for Mordechai, and Yisroel Meir could certainly benefit a great deal from a comfortable home with plenty of food. Why not invite Yisroel Meir to move in with the Gordons? Reb Aryeh Zev agreed and, of course, the boys were overjoyed. The arrangement was a great success and the boys remained lifelong friends.

For Yisroel Meir, living in the Gordon home brought an unexpected benefit that was to have a great effect on his Torah study. Reb Yisroel Gordon had one of the finest Talmudic libraries in Eastern Europe. Yisroel Meir used to spend hours at a time in the library immersing himself in the wisdom of the great men of past centuries. With nearly every *sefer* he could hope for at his disposal, Yisroel Meir developed a studying method that stayed with him for the rest of his life. Whenever he studied *Halachah* (Torah law) or Talmud, he would start at the beginning: First he would study the passage in the *Chumash* upon which the law was based. Then he would go on to the *Mishnah, Gemara, Rishonim* (early commentators) and so on down the line until he had studied the entire development of the law as it was finally decided. This habit of thorough and complete study is reflected in his later books, especially *Mishnah Berurah,* one of the most important commentaries on Jewish law of this century.

In the Gordon home, Yisroel Meir came to know the aristocracy of Vilna Jewry. He was treated like a member of the family, but he never forgot the simplicity and honesty of his parents. He learned how to listen and talk to the wealthy, mighty and learned without being overawed. That, too, was a valuable experience for him — too many people, in their excitement at meeting with the high and mighty, fail to realize that people are worthy of respect not because of how much money they have in the bank, but how much kindness they have in their hearts and how much wisdom they have in their minds.

Fear swept through Vilna as 5609 (1848) began. A cholera epidemic hit Eastern Europe, and, as *Yom Kippur* drew near, the citizens of Vilna prayed that the dreaded disease would not strike their city. On *Yom Kippur,* the great *gaon* (Torah genius), Rabbi Yisroel Salanter, walked up to the pulpit of the city's main synagogue. He told the people that they were not permitted to fast on that *Yom Kippur!* To fast, he said, would weaken them and increase their chance of catching cholera, a disease that was a death sentence for a large proportion of its victims. When lives are in danger, the Torah commands us to save them — even if it means eating on *Yom Kippur.* The people in the *shul* were stunned! Many were ready to fast anyway despite the command of the rabbi. But he wasn't finished yet. Reb Yisroel took a cup of wine and a plate of cake, made *Kiddush* and ate right there as hundreds watched!

Thanks to his example, most of Vilna's Jews obeyed him and ate. No one will ever know how many potential cholera victims were saved as a result of Reb Yisroel's quick thinking — but there was one person who was not helped.

Reb Aryeh Zev fell ill with cholera on *Simchas Torah,* when the epidemic hit Vilna with full force. He was only forty-seven years old; Yisroel Meir was only eleven. Yisroel Meir stood at his father's bedside and watched as he was rubbed down with alcohol to bring down the fever. It was too late. Just before he died, Reb Aryeh Zev called his friends and said, "I beg you, take care that my orphan should remain an observant, G-d-fearing Jew."

Reb Aryeh Zev's "fortune" consisted of two *sefarim* — they were his son's inheritance. But Yisroel Meir also inherited something priceless from his father — love of *Hashem* and love of Torah.

Following his father's death, Yisroel Meir became more serious than ever about his studies. His reputation grew as he showed himself to be the equal of scholars many years his senior. In particular, he attended the famous lectures of the *gaon*, Rabbi Yaakov Kovner. The other students at the lectures were many years older than he, and they didn't like the idea of a mere "child" becoming a member of their group. Nevertheless, Yisroel Meir stayed on and proved himself to be worthy of a place at the table of Reb Yaakov. The life of the young orphan was made easier by the presence of his half-brother Aharon, a child of Reb Aryeh Zev's first marriage, who was about nine years older. Aharon studied with him, and, even after becoming famous as the *Chofetz Chaim,* Yisroel Meir many times referred to Aharon as his *rebbe.* Aharon was ordained as a rabbi by Rabbi Yaakov Kovner — a very great honor — but never became a practicing rabbi. He settled in Zhetel where he struggled to make a living as a not-very-successful businessman.

Yisroel Meir grew not only in wisdom, but also in piety. Already as a teen-ager he began setting aside part of each day to examine himself. He would go off alone in a corner of the synagogue or for a walk in the woods and he would mention all of the things for which he had to be ashamed and repent. It seems strange to us that Yisroel Meir — who later became the *Chofetz Chaim,* so perfect a human being — should have to repent. But *he* never thought so. He was never satisfied with himself and, no matter how well he studied, prayed or performed kind deeds, he criticized himself for not being better. Sometimes, children used to hide and listen in to his talks with himself, and it was from them that others learned how strict Yisroel Meir was with himself — always striving to improve and be a better servant of *Hashem* and his fellow Jews.

Even as a boy, he was extra careful never to hurt another person. When he was sixteen, he once accidentally stepped on someone's foot. The man wasn't hurt; quite possibly he didn't even feel it, but young Yisroel Meir went to a great deal of trouble to find the man before the next *Yom Kippur* and beg forgiveness.

He used to say, "A sin against another person is worse than a sin against *Hashem.* It is always possible to repent and ask *Hashem* to forgive our sins. But a sin against a person? What if he moves to America! Or dies! Ask him to forgive you then!"

Early marriages were common in those days, so it is not surprising that sixteen-year old Yisroel Meir had many offers of marriage from fathers who were anxious to have as a son-in-law a lad who seemed destined to become one of the great Torah scholars of the age. If there was any city where his knowledge and potential could be appreciated it was Vilna. True, he was an orphan from a poor family, but his late father was a respected *talmid chacham* (Torah scholar) — and Yisroel Meir himself …! One of Vilna's wealthiest Jews offered him a gift of 10,000 rubles if he would consent to marry his daughter. Ten thousand rubles in those days was a fortune. It would have enabled Yisroel Meir to spend the rest of his life studying Torah without ever having to worry about making a living.

He began to wonder what he should do with his future. Of course, he would never marry a woman just for money, but in those days when the hated Russian Czarist government made nearly all Jews live lives of unbearable poverty, a young man could not fail to consider an opportunity to marry into wealth. Yisroel Meir would not agree to something as important as marriage without his mother's permission and advice, so he began to think that perhaps he should leave his studies for a while to consult Dobrusha. She no longer lived in Zhetel. About three years after Reb Aryeh Zev's death she had remarried and was living in Radin, not far from Zhetel.

Then, one day, Yisroel Meir had a visit from a young woman. She introduced herself as a stepdaughter of Dobrusha, a daughter of her second husband, Reb Shimon of Radin. She told Yisroel Meir that his mother wanted him to come to Radin for a visit. To him, his mother's wish was a command. Immediately, he dropped everything and made ready to travel to Radin.

CHAPTER FOUR
Yisroel Meir Comes Home

Reb Shimon was one of the wealthiest men in Radin — not rich enough to be noticed in a big city like Vilna, but, by small town standards, he was a wealthy man indeed. He owned seventy acres of farmland, several houses, and many horses and cows. Reb Shimon was one of the most respected Jews in town. He was a Torah scholar who had studied in the great Volozhin Yeshivah under its founder Reb Chaim, the most famous student of the Vilna Gaon. Reb Shimon never let a day go by without studying Torah and he used to say that whenever he saw people studying Torah a thrill of ecstasy used to surge through his entire body. Whenever there was a serious problem facing the community, Reb Shimon was one of those to whom people turned for advice and help. He was famous throughout the area for his kindness to unfortunate Jews who found themselves imprisoned by the anti-Semitic Russian authorities.

There had been a time when Reb Shimon was far wealthier, when even Vilna would have taken notice of him. But a fire destroyed much of his property and local government officials took away much of his land for public (or their own) use.

When his first wife died, he was left with one still unmarried daughter. After a while, he decided to remarry, but he was also concerned with finding a suitable husband for his daughter. To him, a suitable husband meant a young man who combined Torah scholarship, deep piety, good sense and a feeling of responsibility for others. That is not an easy combination to find anywhere, least of all in a a town with a small population and no *yeshivah* for senior students. When Reb Shimon heard about Dobrusha, then nearly three years a widow in Zhetel, he thought he might have solved both problems in one marriage. Her own reputation was excellent and the stories told about her son seemed almost too good to be true. Imagine — little Zhetel producing a son who was considered one of the finest students in Vilna — the Jerusalem of Lithuania! And if Reb Shimon and Dobrusha were to marry, it would hardly be surprising if his daughter, Fraida, and her son, Yisroel Meir, would marry. In those days, most marriages were arranged by parents and, unless there were strong reasons to object, children usually went along. Besides, in the cruel poverty that afflicted over ninety-eight percent of Eastern European Jews, no young man could easily refuse the opportunity to become the son-in-law of a well-to-do man like Reb Shimon. For a boy like Yisroel Meir, marrying Reb Shimon's daughter would mean the opportunity to spend many years in uninterrupted Torah study at his father-in-law's expense, the opportunity to become a great enough scholar to be chosen rabbi of a city or *rosh yeshivah* in a seminary.

Reb Shimon sent a trusted friend to visit Dobrusha to suggest the marriage to her. The widow and widower met and married — and Reb Shimon tactfully suggested to Dobrusha that an important consideration to him was the future of their children.

Yisroel Meir was fourteen at the time, but neither his mother nor his stepfather asked him to come to live with them in Radin. He was doing so well in Vilna — and his Torah studies were so important to both Reb Shimon and Dobrusha — that it would have been unthinkable for them to ask him to come home.

Almost two years went by. In Vilna, Yisroel Meir was receiving handsome offers of marriage while in Radin, Reb Shimon began thinking that it was time to carry out his own plans for Fraida and his new stepson. Chaya Sarah, Reb Shimon's married daughter, knew of her father's plans and she wanted to be sure that Fraida's match would be arranged soon. Without her father's knowledge, Chaya Sarah traveled to Vilna to tell Yisroel Meir, "Your mother wants you to come home for a visit."

Yisroel Meir had always been careful to honor his parents and this time would be no exception even though the request had caught him by surprise. In later years when he was himself a father and living in Radin near his mother, he never left town on a trip, no matter how small, without visiting her to say good-bye. So he packed his few belongings and came to Dobrusha's new home.

It didn't take Reb Shimon long to realize that everything he had heard about the Zheteler genius was true. If anything, all he had heard was an understatement. Reb Shimon decided that he could find no better match for Fraida and, in a private conversation with Yisroel Meir, asked him to consider marrying her.

Yisroel Meir was surprised, even shocked! Now he understood why he had been summoned to Radin. But Fraida

Chapter 4: Yisroel Meir Comes Home / 43

was a few years older than he! And even though he had come to like and respect Reb Shimon, he had been offered matches in Vilna that far overshadowed even the most distinguished Jewish family in Radin! And what of the ten thousand rubles he had been offered by one Vilna family — enough to live on for the rest of his life?

He answered Reb Shimon, "I cannot make a decision before I discuss it with my mother."

Yisroel Meir went to talk to Dobrusha. He didn't even tell her about his offers in Vilna; he wasn't the sort of person who would sell himself to the highest bidder. Besides, he understood very well that if he said the wrong thing, it might cause friction between Dobrusha and Reb Shimon, and he would do nothing to cause his mother unhappiness. All he did was ask her whether she was in favor of his marriage to Fraida. She said yes.

Yisroel Meir went to Reb Shimon and said that he would be proud to become his son-in-law. Reb Shimon was overjoyed and promised to support the couple for twenty years so that Yisroel Meir could study Torah without financial worries. He knew that he had assured Fraida a lifetime of happiness and that his family could now feel that their dead mother's memory would be honored by the husband of her youngest daughter.

Not everyone, however, was happy to hear the news. Aharon, Yisroel Meir's older brother, then living in Zhetel, was horrified by the idea that his brother, the toast of Vilna, was to become engaged to the daughter of a small-town landowner. He rented a horse and buggy and went tearing along the road to Radin to put an end to the plan before the *t'nayim* (written

agreement to marry) were signed. As he approached Radin, one of his buggy-wheels broke. By the time he was able to repair it and arrive at Reb Shimon's home, it was too late — Yisroel Meir and Fraida were engaged! Aharon wouldn't give up. He insisted that his brother break the engagement, but Yisroel Meir wouldn't hear of it.

As he and Reb Shimon had agreed, Yisroel Meir returned to Vilna for one more year of study before the marriage. During that year Reb Shimon's fortunes plunged. When the year began he was a happy, fairly wealthy man. When it ended, he and his family knew the meaning of hunger.

It began when the local governor ordered that the substantial landowners among Radin's Jews surrender nearly all of their land to the government. Seven people were affected. They knew that they could expect no sympathy from the governor; he was a notorious anti-Semite whose decision was based on hatred, not justice. They decided to send a representative to St. Petersburg, capital of Russia, to plead with the royal minister, to go to Czar Nikolai himself, if necessary. To prove their case, the Jews had three-hundred-year old documents proving that the land was theirs. Naturally, the man chosen to go to St. Petersburg was Reb Shimon and, naturally, he refused to accept any money from his fellow townspeople to help pay for his expenses! The trip and living expenses in the capital cost him a small fortune — and the mission ended in failure. He appeared before the Czar, who admitted that the land had been Jewish for centuries, but added that many changes had taken place during that time — so the ownership of the land could also change.

Reb Shimon returned home empty-handed. His land was taken and divided up for distribution to the gentiles of Radin. He received not a penny for it. There was one consolation, however. One section of the land was supposed to go to a neighbor of his. Upon being given the deed to the land, the man came to Reb Shimon and said, "I cannot take your land and see you left with nothing. Take it back." The gentile's kindness was far more important than even he realized at the time. Many years later when the *Chofetz Chaim* sought a plot upon which to build his *yeshivah,* his son-in-law bought that very same plot from his cousins, the heirs of Reb Shimon. The man who loved Torah so much — Reb Shimon — was given back part of his fortune — surely by heavenly intervention — so that a great house of Torah could be built upon it.

His misfortunes were not yet done. An angry Czarist official came to visit him and accused him of disloyalty to his country because he so often assisted people "accused" of crimes. In a way, he was right; Reb Shimon was well-known as the one man in the area who would always try to assist Jewish defendants. In those days, Jews were often arrested on false charges. Even if the charge happened to be true, a Jew would always be punished far more than he deserved. Reb Shimon had always gone out of his way to help such people. Naturally the corrupt Russian officials were angry at his meddling. But how could this mean that he was disloyal?

His visitor brushed aside all his protests. "If you ever again try to get a Jew out of jail you will be arrested and sent to Siberia to die!" he roared.

Soon afterward a Jew came to Reb Shimon and asked him to intercede for his son, a thief who had been caught and jailed. Reb Shimon explained that he was powerless, that if he tried to help, not only would the prisoner remain in prison, but he, Reb Shimon, would be arrested and condemned to a fate worse than death. All his explanations were to no avail. The man became infuriated and shouted a threat, "If you do not help my son, then my comrades and I will burn down your buildings."

Reb Shimon was helpless. He couldn't help them and he couldn't prevent them from carrying out their threats. Within days he was left with only one small house to use as living quarters for his family.

Then disease struck his herds and all of his cows and horses died. That left him without animals to pull his plow and without a source of manure for his fertilizer. As a result the summer's crop was very small.

Not surprisingly, Yisroel Meir's relatives again urged him to break the engagement. Now he was certainly entitled to do so, they argued, because Reb Shimon could not keep the financial commitments he had made to the young couple. What right did

Yisroel Meir have to tie himself down to a life of poverty when he could have assured himself comfort and career by remaining in Vilna? Of course he felt sorry for Reb Shimon — so did everyone else! But that didn't mean he should throw away his future. That wouldn't bring back Reb Shimon's fortune, would it?

None of the arguments swayed Yisroel Meir. He wouldn't think of breaking a promise because of money or lack of it — and that was a course he followed for the rest of his life. Besides, Fraida was an orphan — she had no mother — how could he break her heart by walking out on the engagement?

So Yisroel Meir came to Radin as planned, and preparations for the wedding were begun. There weren't many preparations to make because Reb Shimon hadn't the money to pay for anything but the simplest and plainest of weddings. At least there would be enough bread for the feast because Reb Shimon had stored a barrel of flour. A few days before the wedding the barrel was opened — and it was unusable; rats had somehow gotten inside and ruined the flour. It was the final blow to the wonderful man of Radin, but Reb Shimon's sorrow was eased by the priceless treasure that became part of his family. His new son-in-law, now *Reb* Yisroel Meir Kagan of Radin, would become the most famous, most beloved Jewish leader in the world.

The idea of marrying for money was always popular among many people and it still is. But the *Chofetz Chaim* was against it, not only for himself but for his children. He *feared* wealth, because money brings obligations and worries that poor people don't have. The *Chofetz Chaim* could have become wealthy if he had wanted to; he didn't want to. Other things were always far more important to him than the style of his clothing or the variety of his menu.

When his oldest son, Leib, was preparing for his own wedding, he and his mother went together to a tailor to choose material for a suit. As was customary, the tailor blessed the *chassan* (groom) and wished him a life of happiness, wealth, and comfort. Fraida angrily shot back, "Who asked you for such worthless blessings? Why don't you wish him that he become a great Torah scholar!"

Leib, like his father, could have married into wealth and nearly did. Once he received a letter from his father, who was then out of town, telling him that he should expect the head of the Radin Jewish community to introduce him to a very fine Jew who would discuss with him the possibility of becoming engaged to his daughter. The *Chofetz Chaim* asked that Leib listen courteously, but that he make some excuse and not consider the offer. Leib was very puzzled when he met the man in question. He was a very fine person, a wealthy businessman and scholar with an excellent reputation for honesty and observance of *mitzvos*. Why, Leib wondered, was his father opposed to the match? Surely it was unfair to assume that all wealthy people must be bad!

Several years later, when Reb Leib was already happily married, the *Chofetz Chaim* wrote him saying that the entire family should thank *Hashem* for saving them from misfortune. The man about whom the *Chofetz Chaim* had cautioned Reb Leib had had a tragedy in his family. He had sent his younger daughter to study in a non-Jewish secondary school in the large city of Grodno. There, away from her family, she had fallen in love with a Polish army officer and converted to Christianity to marry him. Her father rushed there to try to reason with her, but to no avail.

The *Chofetz Chaim* concluded his letter, "How great has been the Heavenly mercy to us in preventing us from making a terrible mistake. Where would we have hidden in our humiliation if we had married into that family? Worst of all, we would have become an embarrassment for all Torah scholars — people would be saying that Torah scholars are ready to become part of any family or do anything if the price is right."

During the winter of 5642 (1882), the *Chofetz Chaim* wrote Reb Leib asking him to meet him in Bialystok, where he was busy selling his *sefarim*. There was a young man named Aharon in Bialystok who went out of his way to assist the *Chofetz Chaim*, and the sage felt that Aharon would be a suitable match for his daughter. Before the *Chofetz Chaim* discussed the matter with Aharon, he wanted to get Reb Leib's opinion of the young man. Reb Leib became friendly with Aharon and thought he would make a fine husband for his sister. Then the *Chofetz Chaim* sent Reb Leib to Grodna to find out about Aharon's family. They turned out to be very fine, but very poor, people. Aside from their little home, they owned a shack worth about one hundred rubles that they planned to sell to provide a wedding gift for their son. Otherwise, Aharon's father barely earned enough as a baker to feed himself and his wife.

The family's poverty didn't interest the *Chofetz Chaim* a bit. Aharon was a fine young man. His parents were kind, generous,

G-d-fearing people. The match was suitable.

And as for the *Chofetz Chaim* himself? — did he ever wonder whether his life would have been easier or more productive had he married the very wealthy girl from Vilna, instead of Fraida, from a poor family in little Radin?

Reb Leib recalled hearing his father say quite often, "The little bit of Torah that I have is thanks to your mother, because she was satisfied with dry bread and never asked for nice clothes or beautiful furniture and the like.

"What would have become of me had I not married your mother?

"What would have become of me had I taken the ten thousand rubles in Vilna?"

CHAPTER FIVE
A Life Takes Shape

Reb Yisroel Meir and Fraida set up house in Radin. He was only seventeen years old at the time, and despite the extreme poverty of Reb Shimon's family during those difficult years, there was no question in anyone's mind that every possible effort must be made to enable him to continue his Torah studies. For him, poverty was no obstacle. He had known hunger in Vilna and it had not slowed his progress; Radin would be no different. It is, perhaps, more remarkable that Fraida, who had grown up in a well-to-do home, was equally ready to make such sacrifices. Was it because she sensed that her husband would one day be one of the greatest Jews of his time? Undoubtedly the answer is no. Reb Yisroel Meir and Fraida knew that Torah study is the greatest of all *mitzvos* and that every person must do everything he possibly can to devote himself to it. Greatness may or may not come, but the commandment to study remains.

There were some, however, who prophesied big things for the young man of Radin. Reb Yisroel Salanter, the brilliant Torah sage who founded the *Mussar* movement, said of Reb Yisroel Meir when he was about twenty years old, "*Hashem* has prepared a leader for the next generation."

So Reb Yisroel Meir had two homes, the house where his family lived and the *Bais Hamidrash* (study hall) — and he spent most of his time in the study hall. In fact he used to sleep in the *Bais Hamidrash* most nights so that he could spend every available minute at his *sefarim*.

The local *Bais Hamidrash* in Jewish towns of old was far different than today's synagogues. There were countless poor Jews in those days who had nowhere to go. They would often travel from town to town looking for work or, if there was no choice, accepting charity and sleeping in the local *Bais Hamidrash*. There would also be students and older men who spent most of their days and nights in the *Bais Hamidrash,* partly because their homes were too small and crowded to allow them to study in peace, partly because few families could afford the necessary *sefarim,* and partly because the *Bais Hamidrash* offered a holy atmosphere and companionship of scholars that were available nowhere else. It was not always thus in Radin. Before Reb Yisroel Meir arrived, the *Bais Hamidrash* used to be closed all day, but he changed that for good.

The word spread in Radin that Reb Shimon's new son-in-law was the greatest *masmid* (person especially diligent in his Torah studies) in the *Bais Hamidrash*. As a result, the women of Radin began bringing him precious treasures — candles. There was no electric lighting, of course, so the only way to study during the long nights was to have a steady supply of candles. Most Jews in Eastern Europe knew little Torah — as a rule, boys would have to go to work before their *bar mitzvah* to help support their families — but most people had great respect for Torah scholars and felt proud if they could somehow have a share in their studies. Mothers used to sing their babies to sleep with a lullaby that went, *"Torah vest du lernen, dos iz di beste s'choireh"* (Torah you will learn, that is the best occupation). So when people heard

about Reb Yisroel Meir, the young man who spent his days and nights studying Torah and slept only when he was exhausted, they brought him their candles. And when a man came home at night, worn out from a day's work, he and his wife could derive satisfaction in the knowledge that Torah was being studied by Reb Yisroel Meir Kagan, in part thanks to them!

And Reb Yisroel Meir? He was not the sort of person who considered himself better than the common people; he considered himself no better than them, only more fortunate. He encouraged the working men of Radin to come to the *Bais Hamidrash* every evening to study Torah and he volunteered to teach them. He organized a study group in *Chayei Adam* (a *sefer* that teaches the laws governing the daily life of a Jew) that he personally taught for twenty-eight years except for the times that he was out of town. Reb Yisroel Meir had the rare knack of making difficult subjects simple and interesting enough for anyone, and he spiced his classes with observations on how even the simplest, poorest Jew could improve himself.

If any people were disturbed by Reb Yisroel Meir's learning and teaching habits in those days, they were his mother and wife, not because he was so busy studying and helping others, but because he had no time left for himself.

Dobrusha gave him two feather cushions to use in the *Bais Hamidrash* when he lay down on a bench to take a nap. Every once in a while she would come to take the pillowcase to be washed. Once she came to get the pillowcase — and learned to her surprise that Reb Yisroel Meir no longer had the cushions! He had heard that an orphan girl was engaged and the women of Radin were collecting feathers and material to make her a trousseau. Yisroel Meir, too, made a contribution — his pillows.

Fraida used to bring him a hot supper every night. Since he was usually engrossed in his studies, he would generally ask her to put it on the wood oven of the *Bais Hamidrash*. What she did not know was that he usually gave most or all of it to traveling beggars who had nothing to eat. One night, Reb Yisroel Meir was alone and so occupied with his studies that he forgot all about the pot of food that was roasting on the oven. Fraida came in the morning to take home the "empty" pot for cleaning and saw that the food was not only uneaten, but ruined.

She was angry and said, "Yisroel Meir, if you don't come home every night for supper, I will never bring you food again."

He agreed and put his time at home to good use. He would write his Torah comments at home where no one could see him. In his modesty he did not want onlookers to know what an accomplished scholar he was.

His relatives wanted him to accept a post as rabbi of a town, but he wouldn't hear of it. All his life he refused to accept an official position as a rabbi or *rosh yeshivah* (seminary dean). There was only one brief period when he made an exception to this rule — and he regretted it afterwards. It happened when he was already a famous and respected author and *tzaddik*. By that time he was already considered the "unofficial" rabbi of Radin and most of the town's problems seemed to end up with him for a solution. The community leaders begged him to accept the vacant post of town rabbi. Reluctantly he agreed on three conditions: (1) That he receive no salary; (2) That he be allowed two years to study the areas of *Halachah* (Torah law) that a rabbi is often called upon to rule on (a very good example of his modesty: there was no doubt in anyone's mind but his that he was as expert in *Halachah* as were the overwhelming majority of rabbis); and (3) That the townspeople agree to accept his decisions. The reason for the last condition was the heartbreak he felt at the lack of respect on the part of some Jews for rabbinical decisions. Rabbinical courts had no police power and, if they didn't have the loyalty of the people, there was no way they could be expected to perform their responsibilities. Radin immediately agreed to all three conditions.

Only a few months after the *Chofetz Chaim* assumed the position as Rabbi of Radin, he was called upon to decide a dispute between two Jewish businessmen. He ruled in favor of one — and the loser absolutely refused to obey his decision! Without delay, the *Chofetz Chaim* informed the town that he could no longer continue as its rabbi.

After the first few years of marriage, Reb Yisroel Meir decided that he should leave Radin and study elsewhere. He had a double purpose in doing so: he wanted the opportunity to study uninterruptedly without the distraction of family or town, and he wanted to spend time in the company of older rabbis whom he admired and wanted to learn from.

The first place he went to was Vilna, the great Torah center where he had grown up. While he was there he often went to speak to the revered *gaon,* Reb Yisroel Salanter. When the *Chofetz Chaim* was an old man he once told his son-in-law, Reb Mendel Zaks.

"When I was young, I still thought about ways to serve *Hashem* better and I used to go to Reb Yisroel Salanter to talk about fear of G-d. Now … I am happy if I can *daven* properly."

There was a quiet, saintly man in Vilna whom the young Reb Yisroel Meir admired greatly. His name was Reb Shimon Kaftan, and the *Chofetz Chaim* kept a picture of him in his drawer for the rest of his life. Reb Shimon used to walk around Vilna with a charity box collecting money for poor people. As he walked through the streets and shops he would sing, *"Vehr s'git a groschen gelt, der hot di emes'eh velt"* (whoever gives a little money [for charity], that person has the true world). Reb Shimon supported himself by rubbing tobacco leaves at night. Other *tzaddikim* whose pictures the *Chofetz Chaim* treasured were Reb Mordechai Lider and Reb Nochum'keh Horodner. When his children and grandchildren came across the pictures and asked who those people were, the *Chofetz Chaim* would tell about them and conclude *"Kinderlach* (children), you have no idea what great Jews those people were. They were hidden *tzaddikim."*

Of Reb Nochum'keh whom he especially loved, the *Chofetz Chaim* said, "Reb Nochum'keh reached the highest level of kindness that any human being can attain."

The examples of goodness and kindness that he learned from those "hidden *tzaddikim"* were not lost on him. One Friday night in Radin he came home with a homeless guest. Fraida saw them coming through the windows and she was horrified. How could she feed a guest — she didn't even have enough food for herself and her husband! In her despair she fainted. The *Chofetz Chaim* came in with his guest. Not seeing Fraida, he investigated and found her unconscious on the bedroom floor. He revived her and put her to bed. Then, he served his guest most of his own portion.

When he was an old man, the *Chofetz Chaim* had a student staying overnight with him. His guest was Reb Zalman Sorotzkin

who later became rabbi of Lutzk and then one of the most important Torah leaders in Israel. The *Chofetz Chaim* himself began making the bed for his young guest. Reb Zalman was shocked and insisted that the sage not lower himself so — he would make the bed himself! Seeing how upset he was, the *Chofetz Chaim* withdrew from the bed. The next morning in the *Bais Hamidrash,* as Reb Zalman prepared to don his *tefillin* for the morning prayers, the *Chofetz Chaim* walked over to the young man and said, "Please don't bother putting on *tefillin* — allow me to put them on instead." What he was doing in his gentle, humorous manner was to show Reb Zalman that tending to a guest is nothing to be ashamed of; it is a *mitzvah* just like putting on *tefillin*. And *hachnasas orchim* (accommodating guests) is a *mitzvah* of the host, a *mitzvah* the *Chofetz Chaim* performed with happiness and pride.

While he was away from home, he supported himself by teaching and was usually able to save up enough money to send home to Fraida from time to time. It was typical of him, however, that one year as he was preparing to go home to Radin for *Pesach* with fifty rubles, he heard about a poor orphan girl whose wedding preparations were delayed because of a lack of money. He promptly gave away the entire fifty rubles to those who were collecting funds for her.

He was always ready to help others, but he never accepted a penny for himself that he hadn't earned. The workingmen in Radin whom he faithfully taught morning and evening knew how poor he was and they chipped in every Friday to help Fraida cover the *Shabbos* expenses and have a little left over for the rest of the week. This was all done without her husband's knowledge, of course. He was always strongly opposed to accepting gifts. Once she asked him what harm there was in accepting a gift if someone was anxious to give it. As he often did, he turned aside her question with a smile.

"People want to give me things because I don't accept gifts. If I start accepting their offers they won't want to give me things anymore, so what difference does it make?"

There was one tragic year during that period. At the age of about twenty-two, he was teaching a group of senior students in Minsk when he got a severe headache. Day after day the headache got worse and, in desperation, he went to a leading doctor. The diagnosis was that he had overstrained himself through his amazingly intense Torah study. The cure was to stay away from Torah study for a full year! To Reb Yisroel Meir the cure seemed worse than the illness. What could be worse than closing his beloved *sefarim* for a year? But, as he often said, a human being has to prepare himself to be productive for a full lifetime and, if he could overcome his illness by a year of rest, then it was well worth it. Sadly he returned to Radin to rest, wait, pray, and hope.

During his illness, he sent a letter to his beloved mentor, Reb Nochum'keh Horodner. It said:

> I beg of you, revered rabbi, that in your goodness you pray to *Hashem* for me; that He may strengthen me so that I may serve Him truly and wholeheartedly. I know how little I am worth because I am a sinner. From one who writes with a broken, pained heart,
>
> Yisroel Meir ben Aryeh Zev Hakohain of Radin

Reb Nochum'keh treasured the letter and always carried it with him.

The year over, Reb Yisroel Meir gradually began studying again until he was ready to resume learning full time. But he had learned a lesson. For the rest of his life he used to stop and rest after three to four hours of study, and, when he had his own *yeshivah* in Radin, he used to keep careful watch over the health of his students as well.

CHAPTER SIX
The Businessman

About five years after his marriage, Reb Yisroel Meir was told that his father's sister had died. The old widow had no children and she left a will stating that she wanted most of her money, 150 rubles, to go to her nephew, Yisroel Meir, because he was a great, young *talmid chacham* and she considered it an honor and merit for her soul to be able to help him study Torah.

One hundred-fifty rubles was not a fortune, but it was a nice sum of money and it came at a time when Reb Yisroel Meir had to find a way to support his family. He used the inheritance to go into partnership with his wife's older sister, Chaya Sarah, in a general store. The main item in the store would be material — in those days most clothing was homemade — but small-town stores had to sell lots of other things too: leather, iron goods, oil, sugar, kerosene, herring, salt and just about everything else that a *shtetl* (small town) customer might want to buy. Fraida had no intention of allowing her husband to become a storekeeper; she, like many Jewish wives down the centuries, wanted to earn the family livelihood so that her husband could study Torah. Reb Yisroel Meir, however, was in the family business rather often. He had a very special role to play there that he could not trust to Fraida, Chaya Sarah or anyone else.

The average businessman works to make a profit, and the bigger the profit the more successful the business. In trying to make a good living and increase the profits of his business, a merchant may forget that the Torah includes many laws that protect customers and make sure that businessmen's profits are fair and honest. Reb Yisroel Meir was as careful about these laws as he was in observing the laws of *Shabbos* and *kashrus*. As a matter of fact, he may have been even *more* careful, because a violation of a *Shabbos* law affects only the relationship of the sinner with *Hashem*. A man can repent such sins and *Hashem* will surely forgive. But if someone cheats his customers, he must return the money he has taken and ask *their* forgiveness before he can ask *Hashem* to forgive. Whom has he cheated and by how much? Usually it is impossible to know exactly. So the *Chofetz Chaim* had a special responsibility in the family store and he worked very hard to do his job well.

Once a week he would check the financial records to make sure that the debit and credit records were correct. That part of the job was easy. Then came the hard part. He carefully checked the weights and measures to make sure they were correct. If a one-quart liquid measure is a little dented, for example, it might hold half-an-ounce less than it should, with the result that a customer would unknowingly be paying for something he didn't get. The weights used to measure solid merchandise like sugar, salt, or flour might become chipped or rubbed down with age. The result would be that a one-pound weight might weigh a quarter-ounce less — again causing a loss to the customer. The balance scale itself might not be functioning perfectly. So Reb

Yisroel Meir made it a regular practice to carefully check all the weights and measures. If he found any one that might be defective, it would be repaired or go right into the garbage.

Then he would begin examining the merchandise itself. It had to be top quality or it could not remain in his store. Once he found a barrel of herring — a very important food in a poor country like Lithuania — that had begun to turn bad. Yes, his wife explained to him, she had bought it cheap because it was not fresh and was selling it at a reduced price after warning her customers that it was not very good. That was fair enough, but

Reb Yisroel Meir was unhappy. Perhaps a customer bought a herring when the store was full of customers and Fraida or Chaya Sarah forgot to tell her. Rather than take a chance that a customer might feel cheated or that someone might become ill from eating the herring, he took the whole barrel and dumped it into the river!

His idea of fairness wasn't applied only to customers. Reb Yisroel Meir learned that Fraida was using a baby-sitter for their year old son, Leib, while she was in the store. That was no problem — what *did* trouble him was that the baby-sitter was Matlieh, the four-year old daughter of the marriage between Fraida's father, Reb Shimon and Reb Yisroel Meir's mother, Dobrusha. He didn't think it was right to take advantage of the little girl, so he picked out a beautiful silk kerchief from the store and gave it to Matlieh in return for her work.

Once, Reb Yisroel Meir noticed that there was something wrong with the little scoop that was used to measure salt. Whoever bought salt that day had received less than she paid for. It turned out that the only purchaser of salt that day was a non-Jewish woman from a nearby village, but no one knew her name.

Reb Yisroel Meir tried to find out who she was but couldn't, so he took a sack of salt and went from house to house in the neighboring village giving a bagful of salt to each family. There was once a bag of herring left in the store; a customer had forgotten to take it home. But who was the customer? In this case, too, Reb Yisroel Meir could not find out the customer's identity, so he gave a free herring to anyone he suspected it might be. About sixty years after the Kagans closed down their

business, Reb Yisroel Meir, then in his eighties, was making arrangements to settle in *Eretz Yisroel* — a plan that he was not able to fulfill. As part of his arrangements he announced in the main Radin synagogue that he was donating a sum of money to the town free loan fund in case he still unknowingly owed money to the families of former customers. This was to follow the advice of the Talmud that in case someone doesn't know to whom he owes money, he should contribute to public facilities, things that everyone owns a share of and gets to use.

It would be nice to report that the Kagan general store became a hugely successful supermarket that supported Reb Yisroel Meir and his family in comfort all of their lives. Such was not the case.

There were times when business was so poor that there was little to eat in the Kagan household. Fraida always tried to avoid telling her husband about such bad news because she didn't want to disturb his Torah study. During those early years he began a custom that he followed in later years as well: he used to leave home for weeks and sometimes months to study Torah without interruption. Fraida must have felt lonely, but when she married Yisroel Meir she knew that she was becoming the wife of a brilliant Torah scholar to whom the service of *Hashem* and the study of Torah were the most important things on earth. When he was expected back home, Fraida made sure that the house looked spick-and-span and the cupboard had more food than usual because she didn't want him to come home to problems.

Once, however, she couldn't manage it. She owed so much money to the baker that he stopped giving her bread on credit. She had to feed her children potatoes flavored with fish soup. The store was not doing well. Fraida was exhausted and upset.

Just then, her husband arrived home.

Fraida could no longer control herself. She poured out her misery and despair and told him that he must stay home and do something to provide for his family. Reb Yisroel Meir stood there stunned. His mind worked furiously and he saw the problem much differently than his wife did, much differently than almost anyone else would have. Most people would have seen the matter in very simple terms — it was a money problem. The store was not earning enough to support the family and the solution was for Reb Yisroel Meir to help out by working in the store or by finding a job. He saw it differently.

A livelihood is given by *Hashem.* There are many brilliant, hard-working people who are poor and there are others who become wealthy even though they don't deserve to be. *Hashem* has His reasons for giving wealth to some and poverty to others. If Reb Yisroel Meir was deserving of enough money to support his family, then *Hashem* would provide enough profits from Fraida's store to meet their needs. Reb Yisroel Meir understood! He was being tested! Satan, the angel of evil, was trying to prove that Reb Yisroel Meir's dedication to Torah was so weak that he would give up his studies at the first difficulty. He stood there thinking and made his decision.

He raised his fist and stared straight ahead as he said, "Satan! Satan! You will not convince me to stop studying Torah. All your tricks will do you no good. I will not fall into your trap. I will continue to learn!"

With that he said good-bye to Fraida and left home without even staying for a meal and night's sleep. Fraida understood. Her husband was convinced that their faith was being tested. If they did not allow money problems to interfere with her husband's Torah studies, *Hashem* would help them. She went back to her failing business the next day convinced that her husband had found the key to business success. She was right. Almost immediately — miraculously — business improved and the little general store became a success.

Reb Yisroel Meir was not content to make sure that only his own business was honestly run; he felt obligated to carry the Torah's message to others as well. He visited other Jewish shopkeepers in Radin and taught them the laws they had to know. He pleaded with them to run their businesses according to Torah law just as they ran their kitchens and synagogues according to the Torah.

In later years the *Chofetz Chaim* was famous as a speaker and writer of letters and books about important causes, but his very first public speech was delivered in the Radin synagogue on the subject of weights and measures and the importance of honest dealings. His first published work, too, was an essay entitled *Measures and Weights.* It briefly compiled the important laws and urged Jewish businessmen to obey them. He printed thousands of copies of the essay in poster form and mailed them to rabbis with the request that they be posted. His own name didn't appear on *Measures and Weights* because he saw no reason to gain publicity for himself. After all, he was nothing more than an ordinary young citizen of Radin who merely tried to live as every Jew should.

His honesty became a problem for him. Gradually the word

began to spread that customers could expect to be treated fairly and honestly in the store run by Reb Yisroel Meir's wife and sister-in-law. Soon it became one of the busiest shops in the town market and profits grew quickly. What was the problem? Simply that Reb Yisroel Meir wanted to earn enough from his store to feed his family, but he didn't want to get so much business that the livelihood of others would be endangered. He and his wife urged their customers to continue to patronize other tradesmen, especially a widow who struggled to support her orphaned children. His urgings did little good, so he asked his wife to open for business only a few hours a day, just enough to earn a living. Meanwhile he made up his mind that as soon as he found some other means of earning a living he would go out of business altogether. The opportunity was not to come until ten years after the store opened, but when the time came, Reb Yisroel Meir kept his resolve.

CHAPTER SEVEN
An Author for All Israel

Reb Yisroel Meir's search for an occupation was a long one. For a while he accepted the position of rabbi of Radin, but gave it up because of disputes among the people. He had helped his wife run a store, but he was concerned that customers might somehow be cheated. He had founded a *yeshivah,* but he did not want to make money from teaching Torah. And he refused to accept financial help from others, because he did not want to take anything he had not earned.

Then, finally, he found a means of livelihood that would occupy him for the rest of his life. It would not make him rich, but it would enable him to support his family without accepting gifts or a salary for teaching Torah. And it would enable him to reach out to the Jewish public and help them become better Jews. He became an author.

Nowadays some people write sensational books to make mounds of money. This was not Reb Yisroel Meir's attitude. The *sefarim* he wrote were all on Torah topics, and were all intended to encourage Jews towards greater observance of *mitzvos.*

During his lifetime, Reb Yisroel Meir wrote no less than twenty-five volumes. This was in addition to countless articles

and public announcements. He did not go searching for topics to write about. Instead, if he noticed a problem facing the Jewish nation — such as as decline in moral values or ignorance of a *mitzvah* — he would devote a book to it. In this way, he could bring possible solutions and forgotten information to public attention.

Reb Yisroel Meir would supervise the publication of each book, to make sure that it emerged without mistakes. Then he would travel from town to town for as long as he was able to, selling the book and speaking about its ideas to the Jewish public. Because the Torah's message in these books was so important, he wanted as many people as possible to know about it. Often he charged reduced rates for his books, even if this meant a loss for him, so that the average Jew could read them and grow more observant. Sometimes he gave away his books for free. He was not interested in earning a fortune from his writings. Rather, if someone read his book and grew to understand Torah ideas better, then he felt that his book had been a success.

His first book dealt with the problem of *lashon hara* — spreading uncomplimentary stories about others. The Torah prohibits such talk, but — human nature being what it is — it is very hard for people to keep from criticizing others. Reb Yisroel Meir noticed a growing tendency to speak *lashon hara* in his time, so he decided to compile all the laws of *lashon hara*. In the book, he showed how careful people must be about what they say, for sometimes even innocent-sounding remarks can turn out to be *lashon hara*. (We will discuss the problem of *lashon hara* more fully in a later chapter.)

When the *sefer* first appeared in 5633 (1873), people noticed something unusual about it. It was called *Chofetz Chaim,* based on the verse in *Tehillim* 34: מִי הָאִישׁ הֶחָפֵץ חַיִּים, אֹהֵב יָמִים לִרְאוֹת טוֹב. נְצֹר לְשׁוֹנְךָ מֵרָע, וּשְׂפָתֶיךָ מִדַּבֵּר מִרְמָה (Who is the man who desires life, and who loves many days, that he may see good? Keep your tongue from evil, and your lips from speaking deceit.) Yet, the name of the author was nowhere to be found!

This was not an accident. Reb Yisroel Meir did not want his name to appear in the book. He was too modest to seek fame, and he wanted to avoid the honors that might come from the book. As a result, those who read the book referred to the anonymous author as "the *Chofetz Chaim.*"

Reb Yisroel Meir went from town to town to sell the *sefer.* Everywhere he went, he said that he was only a representative of the author, and refused to reveal who wrote the *sefer.* Yet, people grew curious. The book won the respect of everyone who studied it, and the leading rabbis of the time praised it highly. Everyone wanted to know who had written such a masterpiece. Those who saw Reb Yisroel Meir selling the book and speaking about its ideas soon grew suspicious. They came to suspect that Reb Yisroel Meir, the "salesman," who spoke so powerfully about the problem of *lashon hara* and watched his own words so carefully, might indeed be the author of the *sefer* he was selling. Reb Yisroel Meir tried to avoid the subject, but the truth finally came out. From then on, Reb Yisroel Meir was affectionately known as "the *Chofetz Chaim.*"

Three years later, Reb Yisroel Meir wrote a second book on *lashon hara.* In this *sefer,* called *Shemiras HaLashon,* he compiled the comments of the Sages on the wrongs of spreading rumors. Unlike *Chofetz Chaim,* which codified the laws of *lashon hara, Shmiras HaLashon* convinced people that it was bad and harmful to be so loose with their tongues. The two books did much to bring an awareness of the problem to the public, and helped make people careful about what they said.

Another problem in Eastern Europe at that time was that of Jews forced to serve in the Russian army. In 1827, Czar Nikolai I of Russia came up with a plot to lure the Jews of Russia from their religion. The Czar was disturbed by the loyalty that Jews showed

to the ways of the Torah. He was disappointed that they did not want to become more Russian and that they did not convert to Christianity. What right did these Jews have to be so different from other Russian citizens?

The Czar knew that there had been earlier attempts to make

the Jews convert, but that they had been unsuccessful. As long as the Jews remained united and as long as parents trained their children in the Jewish traditions, it would be hard to convert them. "But what if we get the Jewish children to leave their homes and their families?" the Czar wondered. "If we could make them a part of the gentile society, then they won't stay Jewish much longer."

This led to what was called the "Cantonist" plan. The Czar ordered that Jews be drafted into the Russian army. Normally, Russian men were taken into the army when they were eighteen years old. However, in the case of the Jews, they were to be drafted at the age of *twelve!* Then they would be "trained" for the army for six years, which usually meant that they would be pressured to become Christians. After this, they had to serve in the army for another twenty-five years. This meant that they would be snatched away from their parents before they were even of *bar-mitzvah* age and forced to live among non-Jews far away from home. There they would have no exposure to Jewish tradition and education. If they ever did return home, it was likely that they would remember little or nothing of their Jewish backgrounds. It is no wonder that families sat *shivah* (seven days of mourning) when their young sons were taken for the army, as if the poor children had died. The grief caused by this plan was heartbreaking.

This situation continued for decades. In 1874, under a new Czar, Alexander II, some changes were made. Before, only some Jews (mostly those from poor families) had to serve in the army for long periods of time. Now the time of service was shortened

— but *all* young Jewish men had to serve, with few exceptions. This meant that, for the first time, all those who learned in *yeshivos* would be liable to the draft. This was a new threat to the future of Torah education in Russia and Poland.

Reb Yisroel Meir, already deeply saddened by the situation, grew even more concerned about it now. He was greatly upset when he heard how difficult it was for Jewish soldiers to observe the *mitzvos* like *tefillah* (prayer) and *kashrus* in the army, and how many were being tempted to marry Russian women or convert to Christianity. He could not stop the draft, and he could not speak to all the Jewish soldiers personally. How, then, could he hope to reach out to them and try to keep them in the Jewish fold?

Then the answer came to him. He would write a book for them. It would not be a *sefer* for the general Jewish public, as *Shemiras HaLashon* or *Chofetz Chaim* had been. This book would be specifically for the Jewish soldier, and would show Reb Yisroel Meir's special concern for them.

The book appeared in 5644 (1884), and was called *Machaneh Yisroel* (Camp of Israel). It contained laws and advice for the Jewish soldiers and told them how best to keep the Jewish traditions in the army. It told them what to do if they were forced to violate some *mitzvos* and it gave them advice on how to observe many *mitzvos* as well as possible. It even contained prayers Reb Yisroel Meir composed especially for the Jewish soldiers to say before battle.

The book was a great comfort to the Jewish soldiers. It showed them that they were not forgotten by the Jewish community or its leaders, and that they were still considered true Jews despite their separation from the community. Above all, it provided them with the Jewish education that they would otherwise have missed while in the army. The soldiers passed copies of the book among themselves, and it became one of their most cherished possessions. Many soldiers who later returned from the army wrote to Reb Yisroel Meir that the book had helped them stay religious during very difficult times.

The soldiers were not the only ones who needed this attention. The Czar's cruel measures, and the murderous attacks on Jews, called "pogroms," led many Jews to leave the country. Most of them fled to the United States; others went to South Africa and other richer, free countries. Of such countries, it was said, "the streets were paved with gold," and the immigrants expected to become wealthy and lead easy lives. As it turned out, the immigrants found no gold on the street. They often had to work long hours — on *Shabbos*, too — to make ends meet. But what they did find was a land of greater freedom and opportunity, where individual initiative and moneymaking were prized. Unfortunately, some Jews were so swept up in the new "free" spirit of their new country that they abandoned the ways of their fathers. They forsook the wisdom of the Torah for the wealth of the market place. They shaved off their beards, grew careless about *kashrus,* and desecrated the *Shabbos.*

Reports of this spiritual laxness reached Reb Yisroel Meir, and they profoundly saddened him. He thought of making a personal trip to the United States to appeal to all Jews there to return to tradition. However, his doctor insisted that such a long trip might be dangerous to his health. Instead, he wrote a book to urge his fellow Jews overseas to remain faithful to the Torah. It was called *Nidchei Yisroel (Dispersed of Israel),* and it appeared in 5654 (1894). Reb Yisroel Meir made sure to write this in Yiddish rather than Hebrew, which he used in his other books. Yiddish was the language used by immigrants to America, and, as always, Reb Yisroel Meir wrote for the average reader.

Still other problems led to other books. Were Jews reluctant to give *tzedakah* (charity) and to offer loans to their poorer fellow Jews? Reb Yisroel Meir dealt with this in his book *Ahavas Chessed (Love of Kindness),* which was published in 5648 (1888). In it, he examined the laws of lending money, visiting the sick, paying wages promptly and honestly, and taking in guests. The book led to the establishment of many free-loan organizations throughout the world. Such organizations help the poor, the lonely, and the needy. Judaism has always stressed helping others, and Reb Yisroel Meir's book helped make sure that this remained so.

Reb Yisroel Meir also expressed concern about the problems of the Jewish woman. He was not one to ignore this very important half of the Jewish nation, and considered Jewish women crucial to the survival of Jewish tradition. He admired their contributions to Jewish education and to the stability of the Jewish home. Yet, he was concerned over the decline in the traditional *tzenius* (modesty) of Jewish women in modern society. He knew that *taharas hamishpachah* (family purity) was essential to the holiness of the Jewish nation. So, especially, for Jewish women, he wrote *Geder Olam* (Fence of the World), as well as two later books, *Taharas Yisroel* (Purity of Israel) and *Bais Yisroel* (House of Israel). It is not surprising that Reb Yisroel Meir's final public appearance, when he was well over 90, was devoted to speaking about family purity.

There were numerous other books, on a variety of topics. All were carefully planned and organized, and all helped advance Jewish ideas. Yet, there is one work that stands out as Reb Yisroel Meir's masterpiece. This is the *Mishneh Berurah,* on Jewish law.

Jewish law is, of course, the backbone of the Jewish religion. One cannot do what *Hashem* wants him to unless he knows the law. As a result, many Sages have codified the laws found in the Torah and the Talmud, so that Jews could follow them. Among the basic Jewish law books are the *Arba'ah Turim* by Rabbi Yaakov ben Asher (who lived in the 14th cent. C.E.) and the *Shulchan Aruch* by Rabbi Yosef Karo (who lived in the 16th cent. C.E.). These are lengthy, complex volumes, which can be understood well only with the help of many commentaries.

However, Reb Yisroel Meir found that many Jews were ignorant of Jewish law because they found the study of the Jewish law books so difficult. Therefore, Reb Yisroel Meir saw that a further explanation of the Jewish law codes was needed.

He went to various rabbinical leaders of the day, asking them to undertake this task. For various reasons, they were unable to do so. Reb Yisroel Meir came to the conclusion that if this work was to be done, he would have to write it himself. This decision led to the writing of the *Mishneh Berurah.*

The *Mishneh Berurah* is actually an in-depth commentary on the *Orach Chaim* section of the *Shulchan Aruch,* which deals with common laws like *tefillah, tefillin, berachos, Shabbos,* and *Yom Tov.* It offers explanations for the *Shulchan Aruch's* laws and cites the views of the major commentators. Reb Yisroel Meir also wrote another commentary, the *Biur Halachah,* which gives additional explanations, and the *Sha'ar Hatziun,* which gives sources for decisions. All of these commentaries appear below the basic text of the *Shulchan Aruch,* so that the student can easily refer to them.

The *Mishneh Berurah* consists of six volumes. It took no less than twenty-three years for all six volumes to be written and published. This was because, as always, Reb Yisroel Meir was very systematic in his preparation of the material. He made sure that he had studied all the important commentaries on the law before he wrote down his conclusions. The *Mishneh Berurah* is now considered one of the essential law codes for all Jews, one which is consulted by the Jewish scholar and layman alike.

Though Reb Yisroel Meir wrote his *sefarim* years ago, many are still as relevant for our own day as they were when they were first published. This is why a number of them have been translated into English, so that the average English-speaking Jew can read them without difficulty. Those who do so find that the books speak directly and clearly to them on very important issues. And this is why the writings of the *Chofetz Chaim* will live on forever.

CHAPTER EIGHT

מָוֶת וְחַיִּים בְּיַד לָשׁוֹן
Death and Life Are in the Power of the Tongue

(Mishlei 18:21)

S preading gossip about others has always been some people's favorite hobby. They love to spend their time going over to a neighbor and saying, "Did you hear the latest on so-and-so?" They get a lot of satisfaction from learning just what everyone is doing, and in making sure that everyone else knows about it. Sometimes they don't even bother to check whether the reports are true. They just continue spreading the rumors, and the juicier they are, the better.

What they may not realize is that the Torah specifically forbids such activity. לֹא תֵלֵךְ רָכִיל בְּעַמֶּיךָ ("You shall not go as a talebearer among your people"), says the Torah (*Vayikra* 19:16). The punishment for spreading tales, or *lashon hara,* is severe even if they are true. When Miriam, the sister of Moshe *Rabbeinu,* spoke slightingly about Moshe's relationship with his wife, she was stricken with *tzara'as,* a sickness like leprosy. It was only Moshe's prayer on her behalf that led to her rapid cure. And

the *Gemara* in *Yoma* 9b says that *lashon hara* was the cause for the exile after the destruction of the Second *Bais Hamikdash*. Obviously, the problem of *lashon hara* is a matter to be taken seriously.

This is why it became the subject of Reb Yisroel Meir's first *sefer,* called *Chofetz Chaim.* Reb Yisroel Meir was personally familiar with the harmful effects of *lashon hara.* During his youth, rumors were told about the then rabbi of Radin, to the effect that his two sons were not really religious. The rabbi strongly denied this, but this didn't stop the story from spreading. People began believing it, and as a result, the rabbi had to resign his position and leave town. As it turned out, the rumors were totally false. The rabbi's two sons grew up to be distinguished rabbis on their own, but it was then too late to help the situation. By that time, the former rabbi of Radin had died of grief, a lonely and bitter man.

It was such unfortunate events that led Reb Yisroel Meir to write his book. Before he did so, he consulted the famed Rabbi Yisroel Salanter. "Do you feel that such a book on *lashon hara* could really be effective?" asked Reb Yisroel Meir.

"Even if the *sefer* only makes people sigh when they read it, it would be worthwhile," said Rabbi Salanter.

In many cases, those who read *Chofetz Chaim* do more than sigh. They begin actively thinking over what they plan to say. This was because Reb Yisroel Meir showed exactly what *lashon hara* was, and how terrible it could be.

The book listed no less than thirty-one laws in the Torah that are associated with the prohibition of *lashon hara.* It also noted that, as the *Gemara* in *Arachin* 15b states, a person's tongue is more powerful than his sword. After all, a sword can kill only someone who is nearby, whereas a tongue, by speaking *lashon hara,* can cause the death of someone who is far away.

It is clear why the Torah and the *Gemara* are so concerned about *lashon hara.* Imagine if you were the subject of malicious rumors. Think of everyone saying bad things about *you* behind your back. Suddenly, you would gain a bad reputation. Everyone would start avoiding you, and you wouldn't have a chance to defend yourself. You would have no friends, and you might lose your job. A few words can have a devastating effect.

In his *sefer,* Reb Yisroel Meir made it clear that *lashon hara* does not involve only lies. It applies just as well to things that might be true. If someone has a private problem, someone else shouldn't reveal it to the world. It is no excuse to say, "Well, that person wouldn't mind it," or, "I'd even say it in front of him," or, "I was only joking. I didn't mean to harm anyone." When someone says something negative about others, even in fun, he has already caused great harm.

Reb Yisroel Meir certainly realized it. Not only did he write about it, but he himself was very careful about what he said.

When he finished writing the manuscript of *Chofetz Chaim,* Reb Yisroel Meir went to Navaradok to ask the rabbi there, Rabbi Boruch Mordechai Lipshitz, for his approval. Rabbi Lipshitz was highly impressed with the book, but he hesitated to give his offical *haskamah* (letter of approval), because he wondered if the author himself practiced what he preached. He wanted time to think it over.

Meanwhile, one of the rabbi's students, a distinguished scholar, greeted Reb Yisroel Meir and asked him to join him for lunch. "My *rebbe*, Rabbi Lipshitz, says that you have written a book about *lashon hara*," the student said. "We certainly need a book about the subject. Why, only the other day I was in the market place, and I overheard someone saying such nasty things about my colleague, Shloimie. I distinctly heard him say that Shloimie was ..."

Reb Yisroel Meir interrupted him. "Uh, perhaps we could discuss the book. I am sure that you can suggest some corrections for me to make."

"Yes, but first let me tell you what I heard about ..."

"Do you think that the title of the book is a good one?" Reb Yisroel Meir interrupted again.

The student smiled, impressed. Here was someone who indeed wasn't interested in listening to gossip. Nevertheless, the student kept talking to Reb Yisroel Meir — for six full hours. Then he stopped, satisfied. Reb Yisroel had done a lot of talking during that time, and not once had he stooped to speaking ill of anyone else. He obviously believed in what he wrote.

The student told Rabbi Lipshitz about the long conversation. That was all the rabbi needed; the young author was indeed worthy of his book. Rabbi Lipshitz gladly gave him a glowing letter of approval.

Reb Yisroel Meir continued to avoid *lashon hara* throughout his life. When someone would begin reciting someone else's faults, Reb Yisroel Meir would grow visibly upset. "I do not want to hear this," he would say, and the subject was closed.

Once, Reb Yisroel Meir was in the home of a wealthy individual whose charitable ways were well known. Unfortunately, the man was prone to speaking *lashon hara*. As Reb Yisroel Meir sat and watched, the man turned to another guest. "Do you know what they are saying about Reb Mendel?" he began. "It's really amazing! I could hardly believe it myself. Wait until you hear this …"

Just then, Reb Yisroel Meir rose.

The host looked up. "Excuse me, Rabbi. Is something wrong?"

"I am afraid that I must leave."

"Why? Are you ill?"

"I am afraid that I am."

"Was it something you ate?"

"No," said Reb Yisroel Meir. "It must be the sudden change in the atmosphere of the room. A dark cloud just seemed to enter the house. Please let me know when the air has cleared again, and when *lashon hara* is not a welcome guest here, and I will be glad to come again. Thank you."

And with that, Reb Yisroel Meir walked out.

Honoring one's host is important, but honoring the law comes first.

Perhaps one story sums up his feelings on the subject. One day Reb Yisroel Meir came to a rich businessman to collect money for his *yeshivah*. He was shown into the man's private office, and the man rose to greet him. "I am very honored to have you here," the man said. "Could you perhaps wait a minute while I finish this business transaction, and then I will be right with you?"

Reb Yisroel Meir took a seat, and watched as the man took a piece of paper. Then he saw the man count each and every word on the paper — not once, but several times, crossing out words with each review.

"Excuse me, sir," said Reb Yisroel Meir, "but could you tell me what you are doing?"

"Of course, Rabbi," said the man. "This is a telegram that I am planning to send. The cost of a telegram depends on how many words it has. The more words, the higher the cost. So that's why I'm so careful about using only words that are absolutely necessary. If I can eliminate any unneeded words, I can save some money."

Reb Yisroel Meir shook his head in wonderment. "Look how

careful people are in wording telegrams," he said. "If only people would be so careful in choosing the words they speak! Instead, they pour out whatever comes to mind, even if it will harm others. What they don't realize is that, as with the telegram, those extra words of *lashon hara* will cost them dearly when Judgment Day comes."

❀ ❀ ❀

King David taught, "Who is the man who desires life ...? Guard your tongue from evil, and your lips from speaking deceit."

Reb Yisroel Meir always guarded his tongue, and he lived for over ninety fruitful years. He certainly knew the secret to a long and prosperous life.

CHAPTER NINE
A Policy of Honesty

"Honesty is the best policy," we like to say. We claim that we do our best not to lie or to cheat. After all, the Torah urges us to deal righteously with others and to be fair in business. How, then, can a religious Jew possibly be dishonest?

However, living up to this ideal isn't always easy. Sometimes the temptation to tell a little white lie is very great, especially if we can benefit through it. Consider the businessman who notices a customer very interested in a particular item. Can he hold himself back from suddenly raising the price so that he can earn a few more dollars? Or think of the student struggling through a test. He looks up and sees the class genius sitting next to him. Can he resist copying a few of the other student's answers? Sometimes it's very easy to explain away these actions by saying that the other person probably doesn't care. Besides, no one will notice.

However, a dishonest person forgets one thing. Someone *does* notice; someone *does* care. That someone is *Hashem,* Who sees everything and judges everyone. One who has full faith in *Hashem* will never cheat, because he knows *Hashem* is watching.

The *Chofetz Chaim* deeply believed that *Hashem* saw every

single thing he did and listened to every single word he said. His *emunah* (faith in *Hashem)* was complete. Those who observed him when he prayed said that it seemed as if he was having a private conversation with G-d, such was his awareness of *Hashem's* presence. He constantly pleaded with *Hashem* to help him improve himself, and to help him withstand temptations. He knew that, as a Torah leader, he would be judged harshly if he sinned even in the slightest way. Therefore he was always careful to remain honest and truthful, even if no one would notice what he did.

After all, he always said, those who cheat to gain a bit of money wind up losing a lot more in the long run. He illustrated this with the following *mashal* (parable):

A businessman hired a farmer to grow bushels of wheat, so that he could sell them throughout the countryside. The businessman was busy, and he didn't have time to count the farmer's bushels. Therefore, he told the farmer to count the bushels himself and to report the exact number, and then the businessman would pay him accordingly. Unfortunately, the farmer had never had any schooling, and he told the businessman that he wasn't able to count.

"Don't worry," said the businessman. "I'll give you a big dish and a sackful of pennies. Every time you make another bushel ready, take a penny out of the sack and place it in the dish. Later, I'll count the pennies, and I'll pay you a nice sum for every penny in the dish."

The farmer agreed to this agreement. As the crop came in, the farmer began placing pennies into the dish. Then, as he

watched the coins accumulating, he got an idea. The businessman would be back soon to collect the pennies in the dish — but why should he get all those nice shiny coins? Why couldn't the farmer keep some for himself? So, without anyone looking, he reached into the dish and snatched a handful of pennies, which he put into his pocket.

He was very pleased with his cunning, for now he was a few cents richer. What he didn't realize, of course, was that for every penny he stole, he lost a lot more money in payment from the businessman.

"This is exactly what dishonest people do," the *Chofetz Chaim* said. "They steal a few pennies or a few dollars, which they use for a little while, and they consider themselves rich. What they don't understand is that, for every dollar they steal, they lose a lot more in riches in the World to Come!"

The *Chofetz Chaim* always kept this in mind. He was especially insistent on never giving the impression of taking something that was not entirely due him. We have already seen how the *Chofetz Chaim* went out of his way to make sure that no one who bought anything in his wife's store was cheated. If he felt that the products in his store were not as good as those elsewhere, he wouldn't hesitate to tell customers, "I could sell you this, but why don't you buy it from the store down the street instead? The quality there is better, so you will probably be more satisfied that way." Some with keen business minds would ridicule this, saying that he gave an advantage to the competition. The *Chofetz Chaim* didn't mind. He wasn't eager for the money, but for the customer to be treated honestly.

Later, when the *Chofetz Chaim* went around selling his *sefarim,* he was equally insistent that all his dealings be as honest as possible. Once someone heard that the *Chofetz Chaim* was writing a new *sefer.* He came over to him and presented him with a nice sum of money.

"What is this for? asked Reb Yisroel Meir.

"It's an advance payment for your book," said the man. "I am paying for it now, so that I can receive it when it's finished."

The *Chofetz Chaim* shook his head and handed back the money. "Thank you very much, but I never take advance payments for any of my books."

"Why not?"

"You see, something might happen, and I might not be able to publish the *sefer*. Then you would have paid for nothing, and I would be holding your money improperly. So please hold onto the money until the book is ready, and I will be very pleased to sell you a copy."

Even when the books were ready, the *Chofetz Chaim* made sure they were in perfect shape. He personally came down to the printing house, and checked the printing and the binding to make sure that no pages were spoiled or missing. He didn't want any customer to pay money for a book with errors.

Once someone overheard him speaking in an agitated tone of voice to his son Reb Leib. When the *Chofetz Chaim* had left, the man asked Reb Leib what the problem was.

"Some time ago my father asked me to send a copy of his latest *sefer* to one of his customers," said Reb Leib. "Of course, I did so. Then the customer wrote back saying that he was very happy with the book, even though the first page was missing. When my father heard about this, he grew very upset. A customer pays for a perfect item, not a damaged one. So he made me promise to send the man a new book, and to check them carefully from now on before sending them out. He insists that everything be just right."

The *Chofetz Chaim* was also careful never to take more than the list price for a book. He knew that some people wanted to pay more as a way of giving him a gift, but he refused to take money that he did not earn.

The members of the Rothschild family were world-famous bankers, and they were very wealthy. Once, a Rothschild who lived in France ordered a book from the *Chofetz Chaim*. The book cost 30 francs, but Monsieur Rothschild sent a check for 300 francs. A short while later, he received a letter from the *Chofetz Chaim*. Inside was a check for the 270 francs. The *Chofetz Chaim* explained that he was grateful for the extra money, but that he could not take more than the price of the book. Instead, the *Chofetz Chaim* suggested that Monsieur Rothschild might want to send the extra money as a donation to the *yeshivah* in Radin. Monsieur Rothschild was so impressed that he sent not only the extra money to the *yeshivah,* but much more, too.

The *Chofetz Chaim* was also careful to deal fairly with the workers who assembled his books. He kept in mind the Torah's admonition to pay workers on time. Consequently, he made sure to pay them correctly, and promptly. Before they began working, he would insist that they be given a contract, in which their salaries were clearly defined, so that they could not receive anything less. Then he saw to it that they were paid according to schedule, so that their families would be supported.

One Friday afternoon an employee of the publishing house was getting ready for *Shabbos*. The man was quite poor, and lived in a shabby house, but when *Shabbos* came, he forgot his poverty. It would be difficult this week, though, since his pay hadn't come through as usual. Still, he would make the best of it.

Then he heard a sudden cry of surprise. One of his children had been looking out the window, and had seen a small, white-bearded man rushing to the door. Who was this stranger, and what could he possibly want so close to *Shabbos?*

The man opened the door, and there, before him, stood the *Chofetz Chaim.* Before the man could express his amazement at the famous rabbi being at his door, the *Chofetz Chaim* spoke. "I know it is just before *Shabbos,* and I am sorry to be bothering you. But I was just told that there was a mix-up at the publishing house, and that you did not get your pay this week. Since I knew that this might upset you during *Shabbos,* and since we are not allowed to delay a workman's wages, I rushed over as soon as I could to give you this." Whereupon, the *Chofetz Chaim* gave the man his pay, smiled, said a hearty, "Good *Shabbos,*" and left. Those who knew the *Chofetz Chaim* well were far from amazed when they heard what had happened. This was just part of his usual honesty.

The *Chofetz Chaim* carried over this attitude towards his relationships with companies and government agencies. Many would never think of defrauding a fellow Jew, but when it comes to misleading the government, for some that is another matter. No, said the *Chofetz Chaim* — one must be totally honest in *all* his dealings. Once again, he taught this through example. Sometimes he received orders for his books from distant cities. To get them to their destination, he would pack the books and send them by train. All items sent by train would first be weighed, and the sender would be charged accordingly. The more the items weighed, the more it cost to send them.

Once the *Chofetz Chaim's* son brought a heavy bundle containing books to the station. The non-Jewish clerk in charge of weighing packages looked at the bundle, and, without bothering to weigh it, quoted a price.

The man's newly-appointed assistant was surprised. "How can you tell how much it will cost without weighing it?" he asked.

"This comes from Rabbi Kagan, the famous Rabbi of Radin," the head clerk explained. "He always weighs his packages beforehand, and writes the weight on the package. I've been handling his packages for many years and he's never been wrong, and never tries to cheat me. So it saves me the time and trouble of having to weigh them, because I know that his measurements are exact."

"I'm not as trusting as you are," said the assistant. "Let's weigh it anyway, to make sure."

They did, and sure enough, the weight shown on the scale was exactly the weight the *Chofetz Chaim* had written. Now the assistant knew that a Jew could indeed be trustworthy, and a *Kiddush Hashem* (sanctification of *Hashem's* name) had taken place.

On another occasion, the *Chofetz Chaim* himself brought a package to the station to be sent by train. There, a fellow Jew saw him and asked where the package was headed. When the *Chofetz Chaim* told him, the man smiled. "Why, that's exactly where I'm going myself. Why should you spend money on postage, then? I'll save you the money by taking it with me as part of my luggage."

"Absolutely not!" said the *Chofetz Chaim*. "Do you want it to look like we Jews are trying to cheat the railroad out of money that is rightfully due it! It isn't worth a *Chillul Hashem* (desecration of *Hashem's* name)."

The concern over improper transactions remained with the *Chofetz Chaim* throughout his life. Once he made a long trip to a far-away town. On the way, he stopped at an inn. There he met someone who was going in the opposite direction, back to Radin. "How lucky I am to have found you!" the *Chofetz Chaim* exclaimed. "I have a most important message for my wife, and I would be extremely grateful if you could deliver it to her when you get home."

The man agreed with pleasure to act as a messenger, and the *Chofetz Chaim* took out a paper and wrote feverishly on it. He then put it into an envelope, sealed it, and gave it to the man. "Please see that she gets it as soon as possible. And thank you again very much."

During the trip home, the man kept wondering what the letter said. Since the *Chofetz Chaim* had been so anxious about it, it must contain some very important news. So as soon as he arrived in Radin, he rushed over to Reb Yisroel Meir's wife and delivered the letter to her. Then he waited with growing curiosity while she read it. Not being able to restrain his curiosity, he asked, "What is it? Is there something wrong? Did something serious happen?"

"In a way," she replied. "He wrote that he had forgotten to close our barn gate before he left. So he wanted to make sure that I'd shut it. That way our cow wouldn't get out and graze in someone else's field. He was afraid that this would cause someone a loss of money, and he didn't want to be responsible for doing that. That's why he was so eager that I get the letter."

CHAPTER TEN
Fleeing from Glory

אֵיזֶהוּ מְכֻבָּד הַמְכַבֵּד אֶת הַבְּרִיוֹת

"Who is honored? He who honors others." — *Pirkei Avos 4:1*

It was a sparklingly sunny day, so the coachman was in a glorious mood. He let the horses gallop along, and he hummed a cheerful tune to himself. Eventually, he turned to his sole passenger, an elderly Jew.

"Isn't this a wonderful day?" the coachman said.

"It certainly is, " said the passenger. "*Hashem* has really given us some magnificent weather."

"That's one reason, but there's another reason, too. I've heard that our town is welcoming a special visitor today. He's one of the great sages of our time."

The passenger smiled. "How fortunate."

"Yes, it is," said the coachman. "I'm just a poor working Jew, and I don't know all that much about Torah learning. Still, I know enough to realize that this man must be someone special. They say such wonderful things about him. He's a master in learning, and he's extremely pious. Everything he does gives credit to *Hashem*. There are some who say that he is one of the thirty-six

secret *tzaddikim* (holy men) upon whom the world depends for survival. I've never seen this man, but he must look like a king. And that's why I'll be there with everyone else to welcome him when he comes. We've even made a sign for him: *'Shalom Aleichem* to the *Chofetz Chaim.'* "

"The *Chofetz Chaim?*" asked the old passenger.

"Yes, that's what they call him. I'm sure you've heard of him."

"Yes, I have, and I'm afraid that you are a bit mistaken. You see, I happen to know that the *Chofetz Chaim* is nothing like what you've said. There is nothing special about him. He is just an ordinary old Jew who tries to serve *Hashem* like anyone else, and who has faults like anyone else."

The coachman halted the coach immediately, and turned to the passenger in a fury. "How dare you say such things about a great person?" he shouted. "Such *chutzpah* (nerve)! If you say one more word against the *Chofetz Chaim,* I will have to ask you to leave the coach!"

The passenger saw how angry the coachman was, and immediately became quiet. Both of them continued the journey in stony silence.

When the coach finally reached the town, the coachman saw a huge crowd filling the town square. They were obviously awaiting the distinguished visitor. The coachman brought his horses to a halt and jumped out of the coach, abandoning his disrespectful passenger inside. He joined the others in the crowd, managing to get a place in the rear. Then, a cheer went up. The great sage had apparently arrived. The coachman craned his neck to get a good look. But all he saw was his passenger slowly emerging from the coach.

"What is everyone yelling for?" he asked someone in the crowd. "All I see is that old, ignorant man."

"If anyone here is ignorant, it's you," said the other man. "Don't you know who that is? That's the *Chofetz Chaim!*"

"You mean … my passenger?" The coachman groaned. Here he had come to pay tribute to this great rabbi, only to find that he had yelled at him instead!

He did his best to hide in the crowd, but, to his dismay, he soon saw the *Chofetz Chaim* heading straight towards him! What

terrible things would this sage say to him?

What the *Chofetz Chaim* said was, "Ah, there you are! I am glad I found you. I want to apologize for what happened before."

The coachman was flabbergasted. "*You* want to apologize? *I* should offer the apologies. After all, *I* was the one who yelled at *you* and left you alone in the coach. But believe me, I had no idea that the one who said those things about the *Chofetz Chaim* would turn out to be the *Chofetz Chaim* himself!"

"It was really my mistake," said the sage. "You see, I was

listening to what you were saying about me, and I grew very nervous. I know that these reports are very exaggerated, and I don't want all those kind words to go to my head. I know I am really no better than anyone else, and that if I thought otherwise I would be fooling myself. That is why I had to stop you from saying those things. Still, I should not have spoken ill of anyone, including myself — even if what I said was true!"

The *Gemara* in *Eruvin* 13b says that if someone is so conceited that he chases after glory, then glory will escape him. On the other hand, if someone is so humble that he flees from glory, then in the end, glory will pursue him. The *Chofetz Chaim* was certainly in the latter category.

Some people search for titles and honor, but not the *Chofetz Chaim*. He never wanted anyone to call him "*Harav Hagaon* (the rabbi, the Torah genius)" or any other impressive name. This was not false modesty. He sincerely believed that, in *Hashem's* eyes, he was just a limited human being — a plain person who had his share of faults. He felt that if others gave him undue honor, it would leave him with a swelled head. It would make him feel that he was extraordinary, when he felt that he wasn't. He always remembered that man comes from dust and returns to dust, and so he must be humble before *Hashem.*

As a result, Reb Yisroel Meir lived humbly and simply. As we have seen he did not seek to live in a fancy mansion, but in a plain little house. He did not cram it full of expensive furniture, but bought only the items he really needed. And he did not spend a fortune on clothing, either. Naturally, he did not look sloppy or shabby, for that would cause a *Chillul Hashem.* Still, he limited his wardrobe to plain black suits and coats, and a simple workman's cap. Unless you knew who he was, you could not tell by looking at how he was dressed that this was the great sage of the generation. If he looked like an average person, it was because he felt like one.

During the *Asseres Yemei Teshuvah* (Ten Days of Repentance, from *Rosh Hashanah* through *Yom Kippur),* those in the *yeshivah* noticed that Reb Yisroel Meir slipped out of the *Bais Hamidrash* and disappeared for a while. Some grew curious over where he had gone. One person decided to find out. The next time Reb Yisroel Meir made his exit, the curious person followed from a distance. He saw Reb Yisroel Meir make his way to the attic of the building, where there was a small room. Reb Yisroel Meir entered the room and shut the door, leaving the other person outside. There was a short silence, and then: "You foolish sinner! Don't you know that you've done wrong! What's wrong with you? *Hashem* is judging you at this very moment, and you still continue to sin! When will you ever learn?"

The other person, listening in, was shocked. This was Reb Yisroel Meir's voice, and it had never been raised in anger like this before! Whoever was in the room with Reb Yisroel Meir must really be a wicked man to face accusations like these. On and on it went, as Reb Yisroel Meir cited specific sins and demanded repentance. Finally the shouting stopped, and Reb Yisroel Meir left the room, not noticing the eavesdropper. No one else came out, so the other person peeked into the room to see what had happened to the one the *Chofetz Chaim* had been shouting at.

The room was totally empty.

The person was entirely perplexed. Only after a while did the realization come: the *Chofetz Chaim* had been shouting at himself!

When he said that he had faults, he really believed it. In fact, he used to carry a notebook at all times. In it he wrote down ways in which he could improve himself and correct what he had done wrong. Therefore, he told himself, could someone with so many personal defects really deserve to be praised by others?

Yet, while he fled from honor, he made sure always to give others respect. Sometimes those who are famous feel, "I am much greater than this other man, so why do I have to pay any attention to him?" Not so the *Chofetz Chaim*. To him, every other Jew was worthy of attention, for in *Hashem's* eyes, every Jewish soul is precious.

It was common for people from all over the world to ask him *she'eilos* (questions regarding Torah law or proper behavior). They wanted to know what this great rabbinical authority had to say about various matters.

Once, when the *Chofetz Chaim* was visiting a town, he came to the *shul* there and sat next to the local rabbi. After the prayers, members of the town came up to him and began asking questions: "What is the law in such and such a case?"

The *Chofetz Chaim* considered for a moment, and then replied, "That is a very difficult question. I am afraid I do not know the answer right now. But why don't you ask your own rabbi here? I am sure that he is most capable of answering it."

The others, including the rabbi himself, were quite surprised at this. Then some of them began to understand. They realized that although the *Chofetz Chaim* no doubt knew the answer, he did not want the local rabbi to be embarrassed. By referring the question to him, the *Chofetz Chaim* was showing his confidence in the local rabbi's Torah knowledge. That way he preserved the people's respect for their rabbi.

Similarly, when the *Chofetz Chaim* prayed in a *shul* outside of Radin, people noticed that he finished the *Shemoneh Esrei* prayer rather quickly. Usually the most pious people take a long time to say their prayers, because they say each word with great *kavanah* (concentration and feeling). Why, then, did the *Chofetz Chaim* finish so fast? "I wanted to make sure that I finished the *Shemoneh Esrei* before the local rabbi," he explained. "Heaven forbid that I should look more pious than he!"

Another time it was rumored that the *Chofetz Chaim* had made a disparaging remark about a rabbi in a far-away city. Word of this supposed insult came to the other rabbi, but he shrugged it off. He knew that the *Chofetz Chaim* was known for avoiding *lashon hara,* and he assumed that the whole matter was a misunderstanding.

Soon afterward, a visitor appeared at the rabbi's door. The rabbi was amazed to find none other than the *Chofetz Chaim* facing him. With great pleasure, the rabbi invited the *Chofetz Chaim* inside, and offered him a warm drink and refreshments. Then he remarked that he was surprised to find the *Chofetz Chaim* traveling so far from home in such cold weather.

The *Chofetz Chaim* explained. "You see, I just heard that a terrible rumor has spread that I had insulted you. I had to come over to tell you that the rumor is totally false. Heaven forbid that I should say something like that about you or anyone."

The rabbi thanked the *Chofetz Chaim* for his concern. Later he wondered why a simple letter clarifying the situation wouldn't have been sufficient. Why the long trip? Then he realized that it was by traveling to his home that the *Chofetz Chaim* could best demonstrate the falseness of the rumor. For when news of the trip got around, people knew that the rabbi must be completely trustworthy, or else the *Chofetz Chaim* wouldn't have visited him. The *Chofetz Chaim* had made the difficult journey only to ensure that the rabbi's honor was upheld.

Reb Yisroel Meir's respect for others wasn't limited to rabbis.

During his travels, he happened to be staying at a Jewish-run inn. He was having a meal, when a big, burly man in peasant's clothing stormed in. The man was apparently Jewish, although he wore no head covering. He demanded service, and ordered a loaf of bread and plenty of liquor. When they arrived, he downed the liquor quickly and tore into the bread, but without washing his hands or making any *berachah* first.

The *Chofetz Chaim* went to the owner of the inn and said, "Perhaps I should go over to that man and explain to him the proper way of eating a meal."

The owner shook his head. "Don't bother. That man is Jewish, but he certainly doesn't act it. He was snatched from his home when he was young to serve in the czar's army, and he's lived with non-Jews ever since. He's forgotten everything about Judaism, and he doesn't want to know about it. He's a lost case, so don't waste your breath on him."

The *Chofetz Chaim* thought otherwise. He went over to the man and sat down beside him. "Excuse me for bothering you," he said. "My name is Yisroel Meir Kagan. I hope you don't mind if I join you for a few moments."

The man looked at him with great surprise. "Aren't you the one they call the *Chofetz Chaim?* The famous rabbi whom everybody has such respect for?"

"Then everybody is wrong. The one they should have respect for is you," answered the *Chofetz Chaim.*

The man was totally confused. "What do you mean?"

"I've heard that you were one of the Cantonists taken into the czar's army when you were young. Is that true?"

The man nodded sadly. "It's been so long since I was taken that I can't remember my parents anymore."

"And yet you survived, and you returned to live again among your fellow Jews. That took a lot of courage, and I admire you for it!"

"You admire me? But I don't keep any of the Jewish laws, I don't go to the synagogue, I don't say blessings …"

"Of course not!" said the *Chofetz Chaim.* "It's been years since you've done these things. You've been in a non-Jewish environment all these years. How could you remember the Jewish laws? Would you allow me to help you learn them again?"

The man looked at the *Chofetz Chaim* for a long time. Then he suddenly burst into tears. "Since I've been back, everyone has avoided me. You were the first to take any interest in me at all. If you're willing to teach the Jewish laws to an ignorant man like me, I'd be happy to learn them."

Eventually, the man once again became a Torah-observant Jew.

By not looking down on the man, the *Chofetz Chaim* won him back to Judaism. And by not seeking glory and honor, he won the respect of all.

CHAPTER ELEVEN

The Helping Hand

If honoring others is commendable, then actively helping them is even better.

The *Chofetz Chaim* did not wait for others to ask for help. If he saw others in need, he went out and aided them.

Why was he so insistent on this? He explained it with a *mashal* (parable):

A fire broke out in one of the homes in a city. Everyone hurried over to try to put it out. Everyone, that is, except for one man, who stood on the side lines, apparently undisturbed by the problem. Someone came up to him and asked, "Why aren't you doing anything to help put out the fire?"

"Why should I?" the man responded. "This isn't my house that's burning. My house is down the block, so why is it my problem?"

"Of course it's your problem!" thundered the first man. "If you don't help put out the fire here, it will spread. And when it spreads, it will burn your house down, too!"

"Some of us are very shortsighted, like the man in the story," the *Chofetz Chaim* commented. "We think that as long as we're feeling fine, we don't have to worry about the suffering of others.

What we don't realize is that another person's problem today will be our problem tomorrow, if we don't solve it now. For if one person in *Klal Yisrael* has troubles, then *Hashem* holds us all accountable if we don't help him."

This is why the compassion he showed for the water-carrier and others when he was a boy remained with him throughout his life.

Compassion really involves trying to feel the other person's suffering. Then you will be more likely to try to help him.

When the *Chofetz Chaim* took his *yeshivah* to Russia, World War I was raging. Jews throughout Europe were sick, poor, and homeless. The *Chofetz Chaim* had a roof over his head, but he knew that many Jews weren't so fortunate.

Once his wife woke in the middle of the night, and found that her husband's bed was empty. Alarmed, she searched the house. Finally, she found him asleep on a hard couch, using his hands for a pillow. The next morning, she asked him why he slept in so uncomfortable a way.

"Do you know how many people have to sleep on the hard floor or in the fields because of the war?" he replied. "How can I sleep peacefully in my own soft bed when so many are suffering?"

That was the beginning of the *Chofetz Chaim's* campaign to find lodging and food for those who had been made homeless by the war. Once he had personally experienced their hardships, he knew how desperately they needed help. That made him try all the harder to assist them.

Often people would come to the *Chofetz Chaim* and tell

him their personal problems. They knew that he would lend a sympathetic ear.

Once a man came to him looking close to tears. Deeply concerned, the *Chofetz Chaim* asked the man what was wrong. He said that his wife was very ill, and that the doctors had almost given up hope on her. The *Chofetz Chaim* did all he could to comfort the man, saying that he would pray for her and give *tzedakah* (charity) on her behalf. The man left looking somewhat relieved. After the man had gone, the *Chofetz Chaim* broke down in sobs. He continued weeping for quite a while. One of his students asked if the sick woman was someone whom the *Chofetz Chaim* had known for a long time.

"No, I have never met her," said the *Chofetz Chaim*.

"Then if she is a complete stranger, why is the *rebbe* weeping so bitterly?"

"Isn't it bad enough that the poor woman and her husband are suffering so terribly?" the *Chofetz Chaim* replied. "Isn't that enough to make anyone cry?"

That was true compassion.

Tears weren't all he gave for those who were in need.

We have already seen how, although he was far from rich himself, he gave away his food to the poor who came to the *Bais Hamidrash,* and his money and his pillows to those who were about to marry. Such sacrifices were common throughout his life.

Once a traveler arrived at the *Bais Hamidrash* on a cold, blustery night. The *Chofetz Chaim* quickly offered him a hot meal, and then suggested that the man get a good night's sleep. Soon afterwards, the *Chofetz Chaim* found the man asleep on a

hard bench, without any pillows to give him comfort. Without hesitating, the *Chofetz Chaim* took off his own coat and put it under the man's head, as a pillow. The fact that he himself was now cold didn't bother him. What was important was that the poor traveler was now sleeping peacefully.

The *Chofetz Chaim* also remembered how sick he had once been, and always urged others to watch their health. Once he was informed that a young man was very ill and in need of constant nourishment. The doctors had forbidden him to fast on *Yom Kippur,* but there were reports that the young man still insisted on doing so.

When *Yom Kippur* came, the *Chofetz Chaim* took no chances. During a brief pause in the day-long prayers, he left the *shul* and went to the young man's house. Sure enough, he found that the young man was not eating. The *Chofetz Chaim* sat down at his bedside and gently explained that this was against Jewish law. Then he took the food that had been prepared, cut it into very small pieces (so that each was less than the prohibited measurement), and made sure that the young man ate them. Only then did he return to the *shul*. When the *Chofetz Chaim* later heard that the young man had regained his health fully, he was gratified.

He also tried to foster peace between people, and especially between husbands and wives. When he was told on *Shabbos* that a citizen of Radin had had a bitter argument with his wife, the *Chofetz Chaim* rushed over to their house right after *Shabbos* and spoke to them until peace was restored. When a man sighed that his wife was making his life miserable because he was poor, the *Chofetz Chaim* gave him a beautiful kerchief to give to his wife as a gift. He hoped that if the man showed her that he cared for her, she would cheer up and stop complaining.

If the *Chofetz Chaim* was concerned with the welfare of individuals, he was all the more so interested in helping the *klal* (Jewish community). The *Chofetz Chaim* considered himself very much a part of the community — never above it.

One *Succos*, it was very hard for the people of Radin to acquire kosher *esrogim*. Even the *Chofetz Chaim* had difficulty. Then, the day before *Succos*, a student came running to the *Chofetz Chaim* with an *esrog*. The *tzaddik* examined the *esrog*

carefully, admiring it. Then he handed it back.

"Oh, don't give it back. We want the *rebbe* to have it for his own."

The *Chofetz Chaim* shook his head. "Thank you very much, but I must refuse. If I take this *esrog* as my own, then it won't belong to anyone else. I would much rather have this *esrog* become the communal *esrog,* so that everyone will have an equal share in it."

When disaster struck the *klal,* he was always eager to help.

In 5687 (1927), a fire devastated many of the homes in Radin. The *yeshivah* building and Reb Yisroel Meir's own house weren't harmed, but the fact that he had escaped any loss didn't blind him to the misfortune of the others in the city. He immediately paused in his studies at the *yeshivah,* and, though he was almost ninety, set out on a ten-week fund-raising tour for the victims of Radin. He visited such cities as Vilna, Kovno, and Minsk, and also went to government officials for aid. In a short time, he was able to raise over 10,000 rubles, a large sum in those days. Not long afterwards, another fire broke out in the city, and this time Reb Yisroel Meir's own house was damaged, along with several others. Again, he went out raising funds, but he insisted that his own family get no more aid than anyone else. Everyone in the community would share equally.

If there was a worthy cause to strengthen the *klal,* the *Chofetz Chaim* could be counted on to take an active part in promoting it.

When it became known that Jewish soldiers in the Russian army were eating non-kosher food, the *Chofetz Chaim* founded an organization he called *Kosher Kessel* (Kosher Kettle) to to provide them with kosher meals.

When Russian Jews were attacked during government-sponsored pogroms, the *Chofetz Chaim* helped form *Knesses Yisrael* (Gathering of Israel), an organization to collect funds for them and spread Torah ideals.

When *yeshivos* found it increasingly hard to meet expenses, the *Chofetz Chaim* was one of the organizers of the *Va'ad*

Hayeshivos (Federation of *Yeshivos*) to keep them financially viable. And when he saw Jewish girls turning irreligious, he helped Sarah Schenirer found the *Bais Yaakov* (Beth Jacob, a network of schools for girls) movement to give them a good Jewish education.

Finally, when the Torah leaders of Eastern and Western Europe decided to establish an international organization that would unite Orthodox Jewry under the banner of *Agudath Israel,* the *Chofetz Chaim* lent it his full support.

Agudath Israel was founded in Kattowitz in 5672 (1912). However, it was only after World War I that the organization was able to have its first large-scale meeting. This took place in Vienna in 5683 (1923). The *Chofetz Chaim* was eighty-five then, and had never before been to Western Europe. Still, he insisted on making the long train trip. All along the way huge crowds met the train at every station to catch a glimpse of him, although he tried to avoid such honors. He wanted to make sure that he could help a group that dealt with the concerns of religious Jews in a Torah-based way. Fittingly, the *Chofetz Chaim* was chosen as the opening speaker at the gathering. (He accepted the honor, he said, only because he was a *Kohain* and the oldest rabbi there.) Though he had to be helped into the assembly hall, and his weak voice could not carry, the audience listened to him in hushed awe. Everyone knew that before them was the sage of their times, and that if the organization had his blessings and heard his advice, it would certainly flourish.

The *Chofetz Chaim* felt responsible even for people who refused to do their share, and he knew how to touch their hearts.

When he was in Russia with his *yeshivah*, he went to a *shul* which had rich members. There he asked for funds for *Maos Chittim* (money to enable the poor to obtain necessities for *Pesach*). The people heard his plea and responded, but not very generously. The *Chofetz Chaim* asked for permission to speak to the congregation one more time.

"I thank you for your donations, though I am afraid that they won't cover the costs of the *matzos*. This grieves me greatly. You see, I am very old already. Soon my soul will return to heaven. There, on Judgment Day, I will be asked to testify about this congregation. I will be asked why such a well-to-do congregation couldn't afford more to help the poor. And I will be extremely unhappy, because I will not know what to say. I won't have any good defense, and that frightens me. What shall I do?"

The members got the hint. Soon the money flowed in like water, and the entire sum needed was collected.

CHAPTER TWELVE
To Learn and to Teach

For the *Chofetz Chaim,* Torah learning was not a pastime nor a hobby. It was a full-time occupation — the focus of his life. All other activities took second place to it.

The *Chofetz Chaim* was deeply concerned over the trend to consider making money more important than learning Torah. He knew, of course, that it was necessary to earn a living, yet he questioned those who made riches rather than Torah study their major interest. To them he told the following *mashal* (parable):

A wealthy kingdom was all astir. The popular prince was

about to be crowned as the new king. To celebrate this event, the people decided to buy the prince a crown — not an ordinary crown, but a *splendid* one, studded with the rarest and most beautiful gems. It was known that a gifted craftsman who lived in a distant city was especially skilled at making such crowns. The people appointed two ministers to go to him with gold and precious jewels. The ministers gave them to the craftsman and he fashioned a glittering, gorgeous crown, fit for the noblest of kings. The ministers' eyes glittered when they saw it. Then they put it in a special case for the journey home.

On their way, they passed through many small farming towns, and decided to stop at one for the night. There they came upon a farmer who had just been plowing his field. Wanting to show off their prized possession, and to have a little fun at the same time, they asked the farmer, "Would you like to see something unusual?" When he said that he would, they removed the crown from the case. It sparkled like a star. The farmer commented on how beautiful it was.

"Yes, it is," said one of the ministers. Then, to amuse himself, he asked, "Would you be willing to trade your plow and your oxen for it?"

The farmer thought for barely a moment, and then said, "Of course not! That would be a terrible trade. After all, I need my plow to provide me with food, but that crown is just a piece of metal. I can't use it to plow my field, so what good is it to me?"

"What a fool you are," the minister said. "With just a little piece of this crown, you would be wealthy enough to buy enough plows and oxen to last you a lifetime. Imagine how rich you'd be if you had the whole crown! And yet, you were silly enough to refuse the deal!"

"The same is true of all too many Jews nowadays," the *Chofetz Chaim* commented. "They know that the crown of Torah sparkles brightly. They could acquire its riches so easily by just learning it. But they concern themselves only with the drive to make more and more money. They don't even bother to trade in some of their time for the chance to sit and learn. Apparently they are too shortsighted to see that if they study Torah and worship *Hashem,* He will provide for them in this world, and also grant them enormous riches in the World to Come."

The *Chofetz Chaim* himself used every spare moment to increase his own Torah knowledge. Even when he was in his nineties and a world-famous scholar, he continued his Torah studies, for, as he said, every new review leads to a greater appreciation of the Torah's wisdom.

The *Chofetz Chaim* knew that one usually learns best when he is teaching Torah to others. A *rebbe* is forced to clarify his thoughts in order to explain them to his students. Even more importantly, a *rebbe* has the opportunity to spread Torah knowledge to a wider public. Therefore, when he was still in his twenties, the *Chofetz Chaim* became a teacher, giving *shiurim* (Torah lectures) in the city of Minsk. Several years later, he became a *rosh yeshivah* (seminary dean) in the Wasilishok, near Vilna, where he remained for four years.

Then, in 5629 (1869), when he was thirty-one years old, a great opportunity arose. The *Chofetz Chaim* returned to Radin, and founded his own *yeshivah* there. Radin was a small town, and its residents were not rich. The *yeshivah* was not located in a magnificent building, and it could not offer its students many physical comforts. Nevertheless, parents in Radin began sending their older sons to the *yeshivah,* mainly because it had one major attraction: the *Chofetz Chaim* himself. They knew that under the care of this great scholar their sons would get the very best in Torah education — and they did.

Eventually, the institution became known as *Yeshivas Chofetz Chaim,* and it attracted students from all over Europe. As the *yeshivah* grew, the *Chofetz Chaim* engaged noted *talmidei chachamim* (Torah scholars) to deliver *shiurim* and administer to the *yeshivah.* Among them were his son-in-law Rabbi Hirsch Levinson, Rabbi Moshe Londinsky, and Rabbi Naftoli Trop. Yet, everyone knew that the *Chofetz Chaim* himself remained the spiritual guide for the *yeshivah.* He concerned himself with all aspects of the *yeshivah's* operation. He made sure that the students were given a thorough Torah education. This included the study of *Mussar* (ethical teaching) as introduced by the famed Rabbi Yisroel Salanter, which urged one to strive for self-improvement. The *Chofetz Chaim* also saw to it that the personal and physical needs of the students were met. After all, he had been entrusted with the care of the students, especially those who came from afar. These young men were now living a long way from home, without any family to watch over them. As they soon learned, the *Chofetz Chaim* was like a father and a mother to them, making sure that the *yeshivah* was their true home. It was as if his students were all part of his own family.

As family, they had to be treated properly. It was the custom

began to study.

He remained engrossed in his studies for quite some time. Then he noticed that someone had brought a cup of hot tea for him and had placed it at his side. How nice of the caretaker to have brought this! He drank the tea, and continued his learning.

Then he sensed that someone had sat down beside him. He looked up and saw an old man smiling at him. "I bid you a hearty *Shalom Aleichem*," said the old man, "and I hope that you enjoyed your tea."

The new student thanked the caretaker, and asked where everyone else was.

"Everyone else has gone to sleep," said the old man, "and why don't you do the same? Learning is important, but you have to have the proper energy for it. For that you need your rest. You don't want to wake up late for *Shacharis* (morning prayers), do you? Why don't you get a good night's rest, so that you will be refreshed enough to serve *Hashem* in the morning. Come, let me show you to your room."

The old man then proceeded to take the new student to his bed, and wished him much success at the *yeshivah*.

The next morning, the student was indeed refreshed and ready to devote a full day to learning. After *Shacharis,* the other students greeted him. Then someone asked him if he had met the elderly man who was then sitting at the front of the *Bais Hamidrash*.

"Oh, you mean the caretaker? Yes, I met him last night."

"No, that isn't the caretaker," he was told, to his great amazement. "That is the *Chofetz Chaim!*"

But, in a way, the student was right. The *Chofetz Chaim* often acted as if he were a caretaker, and he wasn't ashamed to

CHAPTER THIRTEEN
World War I

Poland, where the *Chofetz Chaim* lived and where many *yeshivos* were located, was largely controlled by Russia in 1914. Since Russia opposed Germany and Austria-Hungary in the war, Poland faced a German invasion. The *Chofetz Chaim* saw that a German attack might bring disaster to the *yeshivah*. He decided to copy the strategy that our forefather Yaakov used when he heard that his hostile brother Eisav was approaching. Yaakov divided his family and followers, so that if Eisav attacked one group, the other would escape. Similarly, the *Chofetz Chaim* split up the members of his *yeshivah* into two groups. One group remained in Radin, under the leadership of Rabbi Moshe Londinsky and Rabbi Yosef Leib Nenedick. The other one — under the leadership of Rabbi Naftoli Trop, Rabbi Hirsch Levinson, and the *Chofetz Chaim* himself — began a difficult journey to Russia. They hoped that they could reestablish the *yeshivah* there for the duration of the war.

The trip was not easy. Since it was made during wartime, there were many delays in the train service. Once, the train carrying the *yeshivah* members made many unexpected stops along the way, and Friday afternoon came with no train station in sight. The members of the *yeshivah* grew nervous. *Shabbos* was

growing closer, and they were traveling in a dangerous area. Russian soldiers were camped nearby, and they were known to be hostile towards Jews. What should they do?

Everyone looked to the *Chofetz Chaim* for a decision. It was not long in coming.

According to Rabbi Simcha Wasserman, who was there, the *Chofetz Chaim* announced that he and his family would leave the train as soon as it stopped, and spend the *Shabbos* in the open country. This seemed to contradict the *halachah* that saving lives supersedes *Shabbos*. The *Chofetz Chaim* explained that although danger to life sets aside *Shabbos*, every such danger

concerned, but did not lose faith. "They say that they will keep him in jail for ten years. But how do they know that the government will last for ten more weeks?"

The *Chofetz Chaim* was right. Barely a month later, the czarist government was overthrown, and its prisoners were freed. Still, it was clear that the *yeshivah* would not be fully safe in Russia.

In Snovsk, the *yeshivah* students came up against an anti-Semitic Russian commissar. He went out of his way to make the students suffer, making them work in the forests and beating them when he so pleased. The *Chofetz Chaim* protested this treatment, but the commissar didn't listen. He held the power in the area, and he used it brutally.

One evening, there was a knock on the *yeshivah* door. The visitor was one of the commissar's chief aides. He went to the *Chofetz Chaim* and asked him to accompany him to the commissar's house.

"Why?" asked the *Chofetz Chaim*. "Does he want to tell me of new hardships he plans to impose on us?"

"Not at all. You see, the commissar is in trouble, and he needs your help."

Some in the *yeshivah* wondered if this might not be a trick, or if the *Chofetz Chaim* should really help such a villain. But the *Chofetz Chaim* felt that this might prove to be helpful to the *yeshivah*, so he went.

When he came to the house, he found the commissar confined to his bed, looking deathly ill. The commissar motioned for him to come into his room. "You didn't expect to see this, did

you?" he asked in a whisper. "Suddenly, without any warning, I fell sick. The doctors did everything they could, but they gave up. They said it was hopeless. Then someone wondered if this sickness might not be punishment for what I've been doing to your students. Is it true that you have put a curse on me?"

"I haven't put a curse on you," said the *Chofetz Chaim*, "but G-d may be punishing you for making my students suffer. Now you know how they feel when you mistreat them."

CHAPTER FOURTEEN
A Visit to the Polish Premier

The year 1930 was a hard time for Jews in Europe. In Germany, Hitler's gangs were marching through the streets threatening the lives of Jews. In Poland, the government had its own ideas about its Jewish population. Poland was a country with many minorities; it had large groups of citizens who were not really Poles. The government was convinced that it must "assimilate" its minorities, that is, convince them to forget their foreign languages and cultures and, instead, to embrace the Polish heritage. The largest minority group in Poland was also the most stubborn in clinging to its *own* beliefs. That group was the Jews. There were about three million Jews in Poland; they were almost a separate nation within that country. Their language was Yiddish, not Polish; their leaders were the great *tzaddikim* of the day, not the politicians in the government and parliament; and their children were educated in the *chadarim* (elementary *yeshivos*), not the state schools.

Not only was Polish Jewry strong, it was growing stronger. Following the destruction of World War I, new *chadarim* and *yeshivos* sprang up and a new school system for girls, *Bais Yaakov*, began to flourish. The Polish government decided that it could not openly attack the Jewish religious leaders or schools. To do so would have violated the pledge of religious freedom that was an important part of the national constitution. But it could not succeed with its assimilation program unless it weakened the Jewish educational systems. So the schools became the target of a government decree that was officially aimed at improving the quality of education, but, in reality, was aimed at weakening the *chadarim*.

The Ministry of Education announced that it would require that all teachers in Jewish schools have secular education. This meant that the traditional *melamed* (Hebrew *rebbe*) whose life was devoted only to Torah would be replaced by Jews who owed their jobs and part of their education to the government. Little by little the system of education would be changed and become less Jewish and more Polish. Another law in store was one that would require all rabbis of cities and towns to have some secular education as well. This would have disqualified nearly every great Torah scholar in the land from serving in the rabbinate.

Many were alarmed at these new laws, but many others didn't see much danger. Perhaps they thought that the anti-Torah laws could be ignored as they had been for centuries or that the government would never enforce them. Perhaps there were so many other problems facing Polish Jews in those Depression days of extreme poverty that another law or two didn't seem to matter much. At any rate no one seemed to be able to unite the Jewish leaders of Poland to fight and defeat the enemies of Torah. And unless all the respected leaders fought together, the government would ignore the complaints.

listen to him speak. Somehow he seemed to know what kind of people his listeners were. When wealthy people arrived he spoke about the need to give more to charity. When people came whose homes were not what they should have been, he spoke about the need to educate children in Torah schools and so on. People would listen as he seemed to be talking directly to them and wonder, "Who told him about me? How does he know?"

Meanwhile the *Chofetz Chaim* was busy behind the scenes — and he was keeping other people busy as well. At his request, an urgent meeting was called to be attended by the Jewish leaders whom he had summoned to Warsaw. One can only imagine the beauty and holiness of the hotel room where so many spiritual giants had gathered around one table. Many of them had never met one another before. Never before had all of them been in the same room. At the head of the table sat the aged sage of Radin, on his right was the *Gerrer Rebbe,* on his left the *Belzer Rebbe,* and all along the table sat one great after another. The meeting was brief. The *Chofetz Chaim* said that a delegation composed of himself and the grand rabbis of Ger, Belz, and Alexander should plead their case before three government ministers: Interior Minister Josefski, Education Minister Czervinski and last — and most important — Prime Minister Professor Bartel. All three were important, but the Prime Minister was the most vital because he was the trusted friend and adviser of the powerful President of Poland, Field Marshal Pilsudski. The *Chofetz Chaim* insisted that there be absolutely no delay. He gave the Jewish political leaders only two days to prepare the written arguments and memoranda that must be presented to the government. They were to work on the papers and make the necessary appointments. The meeting ended and the participants looked ahead to the audiences with the three ministers.

It was a snowy, nasty winter day. The carriages of the three grand rabbis arrived at the Interior Ministry and the *Chofetz Chaim* arrived soon after. The target of their interview was not so much Josefski, the minister, but one of his assistants, a non-religious Jew named Suchenik. Suchenik had told Josefski that the religious Jews were meek and leaderless, that his decrees would be obeyed without question. By visiting Josefski, the rabbis would be proving that people like Suchenik did not speak for Polish Jewry. Much to Suchenik's embarrassment, Minister Josefski treated the rabbis with great respect. In an unusual gesture, he met them at the building entrance and personally escorted them to his office. The meeting was brief. They presented their plea and gave him their memorandum. Josefski promised to give sympathetic consideration to the Jewish request. The *Chofetz Chaim* blessed him as the audience ended.

The next stop, a far more important one, was the Education Ministry, the headquarters from which the anti-Jewish law would be enforced. Minister Czervinski, too, had a Jewish official, Adviser for Jewish Affairs Adelberg. He was a much stronger personality than Suchenik and had far more influence with his superior than Suchenik had with his. When the rabbis had stated their case and presented their memorandum, Czervinski looked nervously at Adelberg for a signal on how to reply. Adelberg angrily shook his head "no." Czervinski refused to promise the

looked on as Polish prisoners shackled in heavy chains were marched through my town. They were led by Russian Cossack policemen who beat them as they walked. It was a sad scene and it moved me deeply. I went into my room and cried. I said, *"Ribono Shel Olom* (Master of the Universe), why do these people suffer? All they want is to be free in their own land instead of being enslaved to another country. [In those days, Poland was not a free country; it belonged to Russia which would not give it independence.] Don't they deserve freedom?" Like King Koresh, I felt the pain of the suffering prisoners and, therefore, *Hashem* gave me the privilege of living to see Poland become free. Do you, Mr. Prime Minister, want me to cry again because free Poland oppresses its Jewish citizens? It says in *Koheles* that *Hashem* seeks to help the oppressed. Heaven forbid that you should now persecute people after you were persecuted for so many years. Heaven forbid that you should prevent us from living as Jews!

Asher Mendelson, a religious Jewish member of the Polish Senate, stepped forward to translate the *Chofetz Chaim's* remarks. Bartel waved him away saying,

"It is not necessary. Those were words from the heart and I understood them. Hearts understand one another. All I want is the memorandum. I will study it and I promise that I will try to comply with your request.

"Do any of the other rabbis wish to speak?"

None of them did. The weak, sick, aged man from a small

modern, free world would gain them acceptance into non-Jewish society.

It was not to be. For a while, the theme of liberty and equality for all rang throughout Europe. But when Jews joined the society at large, a reaction against them grew. Anti-Semitism became stronger. In Russia, severe pogroms in the 1880's and thereafter caused the deaths of many Jews and the loss of homes and livelihoods. In France, a Jewish army officer named Dreyfus was falsely accused of treason, and at his trial the people shouted, "Down with the Jew!" In Germany, there was growing sympathy for a group called the Nazis, who blamed the Jews for Germany's defeat in World War I. Prospects for the future were not bright.

The *Chofetz Chaim* took these troubles to heart. He grieved at every misfortune for the Jews — and he knew that there was worse to come. Shortly before his death, he drew his students around him, and warned them, "There is a great menace coming upon the Jewish world within the next few years. It will cause more tragedy than World War I, and it will lead to the deaths of many Jews. But we must keep our faith in *Hashem,* and we will survive in the end." Tragically, the *Chofetz Chaim* was right. World War II began only six years after he died, and it took the lives of six million precious Jews. But he was also correct in saying that the Jewish people would survive it, with *Hashem's* help.

The *Chofetz Chaim* knew personal sorrows, too. He suffered the loss of many of his close friends and relatives, and the death of his beloved first wife, Fraida. Perhaps the greatest blow of all was the loss of his younger son, Avraham, in 5652 (1892). The *Chofetz Chaim* had two sons, and several daughters, but he was especially concerned about Avraham, because, although he was a brilliant young man, he was also very sickly. The *Chofetz Chaim* watched Avraham's steady progress in Torah learning, and he was very proud. Unfortunately, the young man's health did not improve, and he passed away at the very early age of 23. The *Chofetz Chaim* was heartbroken.

At the funeral, he told of a woman whose only son had been killed by the Cossacks in 1648. She was distraught beyond words, but she still accepted it as *Hashem's* will. "Until now," she said, "I divided my love between *Hashem* and my son. Now, all my love will go to *Hashem.*"

"That is how I feel now," said the *Chofetz Chaim.* "All my life I have been saying in the *Shema* the words, 'And you shall love *Hashem,* your G-d, with all your heart and all your might and all your soul.' Yet, until today I have shared the love of *Hashem* with the love for my dear son. Now that he has passed away, I will take my love for him and give it to *Hashem.*"

Towards the end of his life, the *Chofetz Chaim* longed to move to the land of our forefathers, *Eretz Yisrael.* He made plans to resettle there, and he arranged to sell off his belongings. However, there was delay after delay. First, his daughter became ill and then his second wife fell ill. Finally, a delegation of prominent Polish Jews came to visit him. They appealed to him to stay, saying that his presence and guidance were needed desperately in Poland. The *Chofetz Chaim* sadly agreed to stay. "So many obstacles have prevented me from moving. It is *Hashem's* will that I remain here."

To resolve all the problems facing Jewry, the *Chofetz Chaim*

His writings would continue to enlighten them.

His organizations and projects would continue to serve them.

His many students would continue to lead them.

And the countless stories of his righteousness and kindness would continue to inspire them throughout the hallways of time.

מִי הָאִישׁ הֶחָפֵץ חַיִּים — "Who is the man who desires life?" That man was Reb Yisroel Meir Hakohain Kagan, the holy and humble sage of Radin.

The story of the *Chofetz Chaim's* life will live on forever.